CobiT and the Sarbanes-Oxley Act

 PRESS

SAP PRESS is a joint initiative of SAP and Galileo Press. The know-how offered by SAP specialists combined with the expertise of the publishing house Galileo Press offers the reader expert books in the field. SAP PRESS features first-hand information and expert advice, and provides useful skills for professional decision-making.

SAP PRESS offers a variety of books on technical and business related topics for the SAP user. For further information, please visit our website: *www.sap-press.com*.

Vital Anderhub
Service Level Management –
The ITIL Process in SAP Operations
SAP PRESS Essentials 21
2006, 96 pp., ISBN 978-1-59229-103-1

Sabine Schöler, Liane Will
SAP IT Service & Application Management
2006, 106 pp., ISBN 978-1-59229-094-9

Sabine Schöler, Liane Will, Marc O. Schäfer

CobiT and the
Sarbanes-Oxley Act

The SOX Guide for SAP Operations

Galileo Press

Bonn • Boston

© 2007 by Galileo Press

SAP PRESS is an imprint of Galileo Press, Boston (MA), USA
Bonn, Germany

Translation Document Service Center GmbH, Berlin, Germany
Copy Editor John Parker, UCG, Inc., Boston, MA
Layout Steffi Ehrentraut & Vera Brauner
Typesetting SatzPro, Krefeld
Cover Design Silke Braun
Printed in Germany

ISBN 978-1-59229-128-1
1st edition 2007

Contents

Foreword

Enhancing growth and expanding competitive advantage are the goals of many enterprises as they use IT to help increase efficiency, flexibility, and innovation. The basic prerequisite for such a strategy is a high-quality IT concept.

Implementing the Control Objectives for Information and Related Technology (CobiT) framework makes it possible to harmonize the goals of a company and its information technology. CobiT provides measurement categories and models with which to judge stages of maturity in order to quantify achievements and identify responsibilities in business and IT.

Moreover, these issues are enforced by initiatives such as corporate governance, risk, and compliance management, which evolved as a response to new legislation, increasing pressure from capital markets, and higher expectations among shareholders.

This SAP Pocket Guide gives you an overview of CobiT and explains how the tool and service portfolio of SAP can support you in implementing CobiT. The guide highlights the new products and applications offered by SAP Governance, Risk, and Compliance.

This guide describes how IT investments can be used proactively to manage business processes. This helps reduce compliance cost and create more efficient and effective operational business process management, leading to higher shareholder value.

February 2007
Amit Chatterjee
Senior Vice President, Governance, Risk and Compliance
Business Unit, SAP AG

Acknowledgements

The information and list of achievements in the field of Co-biT Controls contained in this guide have been compiled from several SAP departments. This would not have been possible without the dedicated support of our colleagues.

We would like to thank Alexander Ritschel and Axel Hochstein from the University of St. Gallen for introducing us to and supporting us as we explored the theme of the Sarbanes-Oxley Act and its connections with CobiT. We would particularly like to thank Katharina Reichert and Michael Heckner for their cooperation in the areas of governance, risk, and compliance. Simon Bertels, Manfred Wittmer, Meinolf Kaimann, Georg Möschwitzer, Olaf Zink, Axel Egger, Fritz Bauspieß, Tim Bolte, Markus Albrecht, Önder Güngör, Silvia Kniat, Cay Rademann, and Bettina Giese all provided crucial expertise. We would like to thank Heinz-Ludwig Wolter for his careful proofreading of our texts.

We hope that this pocket guide will help you learn about the many ways you can implement CobiT at your company in connection with SAP solutions, to help ensure compliance with the Sarbanes-Oxley directives.

Last, but not least, we would like to thank our editor, Florian Zimniak, whose patience enabled us to realize our concept.

St. Leon-Rot, Berlin, February 2007

Marc Oliver Schäfer, **Sabine Schöler**, **Liane Will**

1 Introduction

Since its publication in 1993, Control Objectives for Information and Related Technology (CobiT) has become a widely used framework for IT infrastructure processes and control objectives. As a result, much documentation and many customer stories and explanations are available. This pocket guide will show you the best way to use common models and standards in IT operations and tell you which tools and services SAP provides to support you in using CobiT. You will need a basic knowledge of CobiT and of standard best practices and guidelines such as COSO or ITIL. The Sarbanes-Oxley Act (SOX), as well as related international legislation such as Japan's J-SOX, have significantly increased the importance of CobiT. SOX is aimed primarily at controlling business processes. This has consequences for IT operations. CobiT's requirements are much farther-reaching and more comprehensive than SOX, however. This means that if CobiT controls are fulfilled, then the SOX-related demands on IT governance processes are also covered.

1.1 Overview of CobiT

CobiT was published by the Information Systems Audit and Control Association (ISACA) in 1993. This organization merged with the IT Governance Institute (ITGI) in 2003.

CobiT was originally conceived as a framework for process-oriented control of trustworthiness and quality in IT management. It was targeted at auditors, IT end users, and IT management. CobiT is arranged in three dimensions:

- ▶ IT processes
- ▶ IT resources
- ▶ Business requirements

IT processes are built and controlled on the basis of the IT resources in order to fulfill business requirements. This results in the CobiT cube (see Figure 1.1). CobiT classifies IT resources as the applications (software), information, infrastructure (such as hardware, networks), and personnel. Business requirements can be divided into the following categories: effectiveness, efficiency, confidentiality, availability, integrity, compliance, and reliability.

CobiT processes are divided into four process domains, which together make up a cycle. The starting point here is the management cycle, as described by Hopstaken and Kranendonk in 1988[1]. Figure 1.2 shows the CobiT frame and the allocated domains and processes. The processes are numbered consecutively for each domain (PO—Plan and Organize, A—Acquire and Implement, DS—Deliver and Support, ME—Monitor and Evaluate). Control objectives are defined for each process to ensure a certain degree of

1 Hopstaken, B.B.A., and A. Kranendonk: *Informatieplanning: puzzelen met beleid en plan*; Stenford Kroese, Leiden, the Netherlands, 1998.

minimum IT quality. The control objectives contain targets for designing the individual processes.

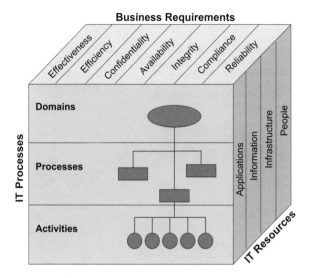

Figure 1.1 CobiT 4.0 Cube According to the Information Systems Audit and Control Association (ISACA 2006)

A portion of these control objectives is used to keep IT-related operations in line with the SOX requirements or the SOX COSO specification. The control objectives were selected by ISACA and published in a document entitled *Control Objectives for Sarbanes-Oxley*.

Figure 1.2 ▶
CobiT Framework with its Domains and Processes (ISACA 2006)

Business Requirements

Criteria:
- Effectiveness
- Efficiency
- Confidentiality
- Integrity
- Availability
- Compliance
- Reliability

ME1 Monitor and Evaluate
    IT Performance
ME2 Monitor and Evaluate
    Internal Control
ME3 Ensure Regulatory Compliance
ME4 Provide IT Governance

Monitor and evaluate

IT Resources
- Application
- Information
- Infrastructure
- People

DS1 Define and Manage Service Levels
DS2 Manage Third-Party Services
DS3 Manage Performance and Capacity
DS4 Ensure Continuous Service
DS5 Ensure Systems Security
DS6 Identify and Allocate Costs
DS7 Educate and Train Users
DS8 Manage Service Desk and Incidents
DS9 Manage the Configuration
DS10 Manage Problems
DS11 Manage Data
DS12 Manage the Physical Environment
DS13 Manage Operations

Deliver and support

PO1 Define a Strategic IT Plan
PO2 Define the Information Architecture
PO3 Determine the Technological Direction
PO4 Define theIT Processes, Organisation and Relationships
PO5 Manage the IT Investments
PO6 Communicate management aims and direction
PO7 Manage IT Human Resources
PO8 Manage Quality
PO9 Assess and Manage IT Risks
PO10 Manage Projects

Plan and organize

Acquire and implement

AI1 Identify Automated Solutions
AI2 Acquire and Maintain Application Software
AI3 Acquire und Maintain Technology Infrastructure
AI4 Enable Operation and Use
AI5 Procure IT Resources
AI6 Manage Changes
AI7 Install and Accredit Solutions and Changes

1.2 COSO

The COSO framework was published in 1992 by the Committee of Sponsoring Organizations of the Treadway Commission (COSO) as a framework for carrying out internal checks and a tool for monitoring internal controls. In 2004, this framework was extended to include the section *COSO Enterprise Risk Management* (ERM).

Although COSO was developed before SOX was adopted, the checks described in COSO cover the controlling measures that have resulted from the SOX requirements. This framework is therefore used as the specification for executing the requirements derived from SOX. COSO understands internal controls as a process that is carried out by boards of directors, management, and other personnel. While these control processes make it possible to achieve a sensible safety level regarding the following aspects, absolute security can never be achieved:

▶ Effectiveness and efficiency of the business processes

▶ Trustworthiness of the financial reports

▶ Compliance with laws and other regulatory specifications

The COSO framework includes practical information in the form of instructions for different areas. In addition to risk analysis, the control environment, control activities, and monitoring, the COSO framework also includes informational and communication aspects.

1.3 Overview of the Sarbanes-Oxley Act

On July 30, 2002, U.S. president George W. Bush signed the Sarbanes-Oxley Act (SOX), a law that significantly affects all businesses listed on American stock exchanges, both domestic and foreign.

The trigger for this new law was a series of accounting scandals at large U.S. corporations. To avoid events of this kind in the future (as far as possible), U.S. Senators Paul S. Sarbanes and Michael J. Oxley were charged with amending, extending, and fixing various laws. The new legislation has come into effect in phases, starting in 2002. U.S.-listed companies are now more subject to the American inspection process, which is intended to increase or restore trust among investors. Section 302 of SOX specifies that the chief executive officer (CEO) and the chief financial officer (CFO) are personally liable for the correctness of the company accounts. The result is enormous pressure within companies to fulfill the SOX guidelines.

External auditors are now required to verify that the SOX specifications are implemented within the company and to certify this fact. However, there is widespread uncertainty about what the initial theoretical conditions of the legislation will actually mean in practice. SOX is not primarily aimed at processes and at implementing them in IT; it has only a subordinate—but nevertheless significant—influence on IT management. Its main focus is on creating transparency and responsibility in the implementation of business processes and their accounting. SOX strengthens investors in their demands for trustworthy information about a company's expected developments and results. This pressure affects the entire C level: CEO, CIO, and CFO.

Since the business processes are mainly operated with the support of IT, the SOX requirements make indirect demands of IT management. Accordingly, the chief information officer (CIO) is affected when it comes to operating the IT landscapes as required by SOX (see Figure 1.3).

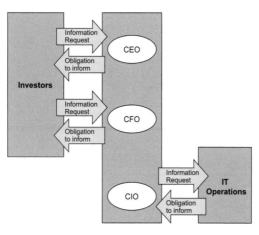

Figure 1.3 Responsibilities for SOX and IT

Content

The Sarbanes-Oxley Act is divided into titles, sections, and paragraphs. Although the law also applies to all foreign companies that are listed on U.S. stock exchanges, no certified or authorized translations of the legal texts are available as yet. Only interpretations and recommended courses of action are available in different languages. At the time this guide was written, SOX comprised 11 titles, which are listed in Table 1.1.

Title	Content
I	Public Company Accounting Oversight Board
II	Auditor Independence
III	Corporate Responsibility
IV	Enhanced Financial Disclosures
V	Analyst Conflicts of Interest
VI	Commission Resources and Authority
VII	Studies and Reports
VIII	Corporate and Criminal Penalty Enhancements
IX	White-Collar Crime Penalty Enhancements
X	Corporate Tax Returns
XI	Corporate Fraud and Accountability

Table 1.1 Overview of Titles in the Sarbanes-Oxley Act

Since the law was adopted, the sections within each title have been coming into force incrementally. The sections described below have particular consequences for business and for IT governance:

▶ **Section 302: Corporate Responsibility for Financial Reports**
Section 302 in Title III specifies the personal liability of the CEO and CFO for the correctness of financial disclosure. Personal liability means that the CEO and CFO also have a very personal interest in ensuring that the SOX

requirements are fulfilled. Because financial disclosures, such as the year end statement, are always made using IT today, there is pressure on IT operations and therefore on the CIO.

▶ **Section 404: Management Assessment of Internal Controls**

Section 404 in Title IV has been binding for large American corporations since November 2004 and relevant for all small American companies and foreign companies since July 2005. This demands the building up of an internal control system with external inspections. The control system should guarantee the correctness of closing accounts and make it harder to commit crimes in the company. The external checks of the internal control structures and their functionality are ensured by the external auditor and management consultancies. The exact form of the control system is not described in the text of the law itself. This is instead described in separate, independent implementation regulations.

▶ **Section 409: Real Time Issue Disclosures**

Section 409 in Title IV specifies that significant changes to the business ecosystem in a company have to be officially announced within four days. In addition, investors have to be provided with information about the expected effect on business forecasts. It is not yet clear what exactly is meant by changes to a company's ecosystem. Would, for example, a planned attempt to take over another company have to be made public? No final effective date has been set for this section, so there is still time to specify the execution plans.

1.4 Connection Between CobiT and Other Standards of Best Practices

One fundamental requirement made by SOX is the introduction of control mechanisms within companies, as set out in Section 404. CobiT describes the measures that have to be taken into account to achieve a minimum quality or to fulfill the SOX requirements. For an exact specification of how best to implement the IT processes described in CobiT, see the following.

▶ **Best Practices in the IT Infrastructure Library (ITIL), or the standard which is based on this (ISO 20000)**
ITIL represents a universally applicable framework for optimal handling of processes in IT management. SAP took this as a foundation and extended ITIL to include SAP IT Service & Application Management, to meet the specific requirements in the SAP solutions environment (see Schöler/Will[2]).

▶ **Standard ISO 17799 for the area of information security**
Like ITIL, ISO 17799 contains best practices for guidelines, methods, and processes, as well as roles and responsibilities, to ensure that information in a company is sufficiently secured. This standard was originally developed by the British Standards Institute (BSI) in 1995 and was called BS 7799.

Certification for ISO 17799 is not possible, as it merely contains best practices. It is possible to obtain certifica-

---

2   Schöler, Sabine; Will, Liane: *SAP IT Service & Application Management*. SAP PRESS, Bonn 2006.

tion in the context of an information security management system, however, using ISO 27001.

► **Statement on Auditing Standard No. 70 (SAS 70)**
According to SAS 70, service providers have to provide proof during audits that they have set up suitable controls and protective measures to operate their customers' systems securely and reliably. SAS 70 was developed by the American Institute of Certified Public Accountants (AICPA) and was first published in 1992. It has since become the authoritative code of practice, and service organizations use it to prove their control and protection methods to their customers. This disclosure occurs via what is known as the SAS 70 Report, which has a predefined structure.

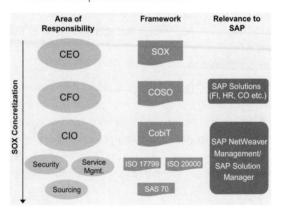

Figure 1.4 Connections and Support from SAP

Figure 1.4 shows connections, starting with SOX and proceeding to completion of the current standards. It also shows the areas in which these connections affect SAP solutions and tools.

1.5 SAP IT Service & Application Management

There are especially close parallels between the CobiT processes and ITIL. However, ITIL focuses principally on best practices for establishing and controlling IT processes. Forming the core of these are the 10 processes and the one function of IT service management. The other IT tasks and processes are described in the books on application management, infrastructure management, security management, and business perspective. The main emphasis of the 34 CobiT processes is on regulation and auditing compliance, along with security in IT organizations. The ISO 20000 standard leads to closer links between ITIL and CobiT, as it supplies the necessary control mechanisms to check the implementation of ITIL. Once the processes described in ITIL are implemented in line with the best practices, the CobiT control objectives are largely fulfilled.

SAP adjusted and enhanced ITIL as part of IT Service & Application Management (ITSAM) to meet the special requirements when operating SAP solutions. Figure 1.5 shows the SAP perspective with relation to ITIL.

Figure 1.5 ▶
Overview of SAP IT Service & Application Management
(SAP ITSAM)

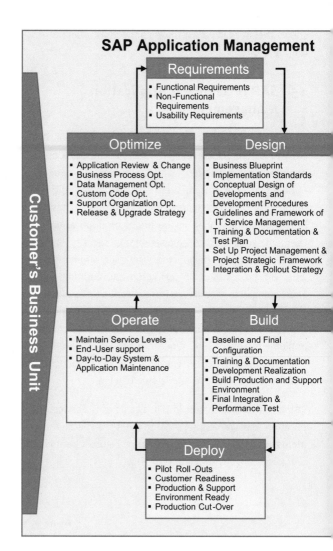

SAP Application Management

Requirements
- Functional Requirements
- Non-Functional Requirements
- Usability Requirements

Optimize
- Application Review & Change
- Business Process Opt.
- Data Management Opt.
- Custom Code Opt.
- Support Organization Opt.
- Release & Upgrade Strategy

Design
- Business Blueprint
- Implementation Standards
- Conceptual Design of Developments and Development Procedures
- Guidelines and Framework of IT Service Management
- Training & Documentation & Test Plan
- Set Up Project Management & Project Strategic Framework
- Integration & Rollout Strategy

Operate
- Maintain Service Levels
- End-User support
- Day-to-Day System & Application Maintenance

Build
- Baseline and Final Configuration
- Training & Documentation
- Development Realization
- Build Production and Support Environment
- Final Integration & Performance Test

Deploy
- Pilot Roll-Outs
- Customer Readiness
- Production & Support Environment Ready
- Production Cut-Over

Customer's Business Unit

IT Service Management

Integration Processes

SAP IT Service Management

Design

- Technical infrastructure Planning
- Technical Architecture Design (incl. Final sizing)
- Project Installation
- Project Systems Support
- Operations & Support Strategy
- Security Requirements

Service Support

- Incident Management
- Problem Management
- Change Management
- IT Release Management
- Configuration Management

Build & Deploy

- Production Installation
- Performance Test Planning
- Cut-Over and GoLive Planning
- Authorizations and Security Implementation

Service Delivery

- Service Level Management
- Availability Management
- IT Capacity Management
- Financial Management
- Continuity Management

Operations & Optimization

- Job Scheduling
- Security Administration
- Application error process
- System Landscape Opt.
- Performance Review & Optimization

Operations

- Job Scheduling
- Print and Output Mgmt.
- Security Administration
- System Administration
- IT Monitoring
- Business Process Management

Customer's IT Department

This guide shows which ITSAM processes are available in connection with the CobiT controls and which SAP tools, services, and workshops can cover the CobiT controls. The connection between CobiT 4.0 and SOX is described in the document *IT Control Objectives for Sarbanes-Oxley*, published by the ISACA in 2006. You will need to be familiar with the core issues in CobiT, SOX, and ITIL, but a detailed description of these issues and their methods is beyond the scope of this pocket guide. Instead, this guide aims to provide you with an overview of the tools and methods available to achieve IT operations that comply with both CobiT and SOX. Relevant documentation on the SAP Service Marketplace, consultations, and other information sources are available to explain how you can leverage these tools and methods in detail.

The following chapters briefly describe the elements that constitute the CobiT domains and the related process. Possible SAP tools and services are listed for each CobiT control, along with explanations of how SAP may be able to support you in implementing these controls.

2 Central SAP Tools

SAP offers a wide range of tools and services for the various IT governance processes. SAP solutions are distinguished by their application areas. An IT governance application is not among these; instead, the necessary functions and tools are fully integrated into the various application areas. Among the many possibilities offered, SAP Solution Manager and SAP Solutions for Governance, Risk, and Compliance make up a central component of the CobiT process mapping.

2.1 SAP Solutions for Governance, Risk, and Compliance

Because many firms use SAP software solutions to map and carry out their core business processes, effective administration (governance), risk management, and adherence to official instructions (compliance) are all central concerns for SAP. For this reason, SAP is adding to and investing in the solutions it offers in these areas. In May 2006, SAP completed its takeover of Virsa Systems Inc. At that point, the existing portfolio of governance, risk management, and compliance solutions was grouped into the newly formed Governance, Risk, and Compliance (GRC) business area. More than 1,000 businesses around the world currently use SAP's GRC solutions.

The following GRC solutions will be used to support the CobiT requirements in future.

SAP GRC Access Control

The scope of a given user's authorization is checked automatically by SAP GRC Access Control. The settings must prevent users from carrying out—alone and without monitoring—unauthorized transactions that could damage the company. The system verifies that this segregation of duties is being applied to all users and across the business. If the system identifies users who, because of their profiles, have many bundled functions, SAP GRC Access Control also supports the removal of all authorization conflicts. This is done either by deleting unnecessary authorizations or, if segregation of duties is not possible, by taking steps to inspect and monitor (mitigation). SAP GRC Access Control offers the option of both ensuring the conformity of an existing IT landscape ("get clean"), as well as avoiding future violations in advance ("stay clean"). Thus, SAP GRC Access Control is a central prerequisite for fulfilling legal obligations, not least those of the Sarbanes-Oxley Act. The solutions are detailed as follows:

▶ **Virsa Compliance Calibrator**
    The Virsa Compliance Calibrator is the core component of the SAP GRC applications. It offers a way to evaluate users' authorizations across multiple SAP and non-SAP systems. In this way, access risks can be analyzed and any bundling of critical functions in the roles of individual users can be identified across the business. This helps ensure the long-term effectiveness of the segregation of duties.

► **Virsa Role Expert**

Virsa Role Expert standardizes and centralizes the design, testing, and maintenance of roles. Authorization profiles and the role are checked to see if the segregation of duties is being applied consistently, even at a role's design time. Virsa Role Expert thus ensures that no new breaches of the segregation of duties can arise during role design or assignment.

► **Virsa FireFighter for SAP**

Virsa FireFighter for SAP makes it possible to assign wider authorizations to individual employees in an emergency, so they can quickly take care of system-critical tasks. In exceptional cases (an emergency), an employee can borrow one of the "FireFighter IDs" that have been issued in advance and then carry out the privileged work using this user ID. All process steps carried out with the Fire-Fighter ID are logged in detail and are made available later for an audit check. As a result, universal access like that with the comprehensive "SAP_ALL" authorization is now no longer necessary, even in emergencies, and the number one audit problem—"super user access"—has been solved.

► **Virsa Access Enforcer**

Part of a company's daily business is responding to fluctuations in the workforce. New employees are hired, employees change their positions within the company, and employees leave the company. In these cases, new system access and users with the corresponding authorizations have to be created, the authorizations of existing staff have to be changed, and staff access profiles have to be removed, respectively. Virsa Access Enforcer accelerates this process using a workflow. It collects all necessary permission from supervisors and those responsible for IT security and checks, ensuring the segregation of duties and supporting regulations during the changes. Accordingly, this tool is used to fulfill the audit requirements regarding authorization management and enablement of authorities.

Figure 2.1 shows an overview of the solutions in the GRC business area.

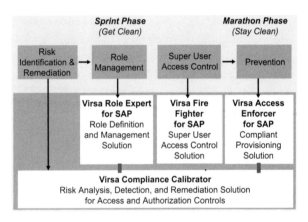

Figure 2.1 Overview of the SAP GRC Products

SAP GRC Repository

The SAP GRC Repository is a central element in the interaction of the solutions, as shown in Figure 2.2.

Figure 2.2 SAP GRC Repository Central Node for Data Storage

The SAP GRC Repository saves all GRC information in a central data store. This includes internal company guidelines, supervisory board protocols, regulations, internal specifications concerning adherence to instructions, and monitoring of this adherence, as well as central business processes. Adherence to guidelines can be administered centrally with the repository, employing business process controls, risk evaluations, and measures to eliminate risk. You also can make cross-organizational guidelines transparent and to display the degree of compliance.

SAP GRC Process Control

SAP GRC Process Control uses a risk-based approach. The relevant control mechanisms are linked with the central business risks and processes in ways that give ideal support to employees and optimize procedures. The Process Control application automatically pools potential process risks within the company and prioritizes the actions that need to be carried out to eliminate these risks. It provides evidence about adherence to internal guidelines, detects any breaches, and informs you of the need for action.

Automated control practices, manual tests, and documented self-controls are included to complete the documentation of adherence to controls.

This combination means that the affected employee takes responsibility for himself or herself and monitors his or her own adherence to the required controls. The results of this self-check, together with the automatic controls, give a realistic picture of the extent to which the organization adheres to the defined guidelines. By using automated controls, you can minimize time-consuming (and costly) third-party manual controls. Using preventive controls also helps to ensure that costly elimination after the fact is no longer necessary, nor is restructuring processes.

SAP GRC Process Control lets you monitor a large number of configurations that are critical to the most important business processes. This includes both master data and transaction data. Furthermore, the necessary manual test inventory is forwarded to the appropriate people, enabling them to carry out the testing and checking measures and document them accordingly. The test inventory is specified explicitly, which rules out the possibility that significant controls will be overlooked.

If the entire inventory has not been covered or the automated controls encounter irregularities, a warning message (alert) and a report are generated. The report informs administrators and those responsible for adhering to the controls of the current status.

To avoid future risks, SAP GRC Process Control can also be used to evaluate future changes to the application landscape beforehand, in a simulation. Furthermore, SAP has formed a strategic partnership with Cisco Systems for the North American market. Using the Cisco network infrastructure will further improve the efficiency of the GRC applications by gradually enabling IT controls at network level.

2.2 SAP Solution Manager: The SAP Platform for Application Management and Cooperation

SAP Solution Manager is SAP's platform for application management and cooperation between customers and SAP. It provides efficient and continuous support for the implementation and administration of IT solutions. Together with SAP Service Marketplace, it represents a central component of SAP's strategic service and support infrastructure. It will accompany you throughout the entire solution lifecycle and offers transparent, business process-oriented information about application management. Although SAP Solution Manager is not a dedicated compliance tool, it offers processes that help you to make IT solutions more transparent, thanks to its broad application-management portfolio, which is one of the main compliance criteria. It also provides access to SAP knowledge, which you can access in three different ways.

Tools
Tools such as Change Request Management, central monitoring functions, and the service desk (which provides end user support) help you to address the tasks that arise when dealing with SAP products and solutions.

Content
The content offers examples (Best Practices) of good solutions and methods from successful projects. These can be used as templates for new projects, such as roadmaps for implementing and upgrading projects, templates for business process, or descriptions of procedures for IT organization tasks.

Services
The services you purchase from SAP's experts are delivered through SAP Solution Manager. The Business Process Management service generates a tool-supported concept, which ensures, for example, that the business processes critical to your company run smoothly.

Figure 2.3 shows SAP Solution Manager's whole function spectrum at a glance.

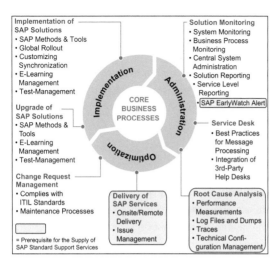

Figure 2.3 Overview of SAP Solution Manager's Operational Scenarios

Implementation

During the implementation phase, SAP Solution Manager provides support with tried and tested methods and tools, continuing and updating the tradition of the ASAP methods. In addition, SAP Solution Manager also makes it easier to upgrade existing SAP solutions and distribute templates that are valid company-wide. All the information from projects is transferred seamlessly into production side operations.

Administration

SAP Solution Manager gives administrators a wide range of tools and processes to help your IT solution run smoothly.

The Solution Monitoring scenario makes it possible to monitor systems and business processes proactively. To run a root-cause analysis quickly when a problem arises, you can target the problem with the root-cause analysis scenario in Solution Manager Diagnostics. Message processing in SAP Solution Manager is enabled with a preconfigured standard for SAP solutions.

Optimization

To improve an IT solution continuously and to adapt it to changing needs, SAP Active Global Support offers services that you can order and receive through SAP Solution Manager. This central access makes service delivery more transparent and reproducible.

SAP Solution Manager's maintenance processes make maintenance tasks such as installing support packages easier. In addition, the Change Request Management scenario makes every measure reproducible, from original request to approval procedures and its technical realization.

SAP Solution Manager supports these scenarios with six significant concepts.

Business Process Orientation

Thanks to its business-process orientation, SAP Solution Manager forms a bridge between IT organizations and user departments, given that all information (such as documentation, transactions, and test cases) can be accessed and administered centrally in SAP Solution Manager, based on the business-process structure. This makes the IT organization's target values more transparent and simplifies the coordination of IT and the business areas.

Supporting the Complete Life Cycle

The lifecycle of an application extends over several phases. SAP Solution Manager supports all phases through its ITIL Application Management orientation (requirements, build, deploy, operate, and optimize). With this continuous cycle, particular attention is paid to the dependencies between the different phases. It is useful in operations, for example, to know how the business processes were implemented. Information about the current status of operations is necessary to optimize a solution. A holistic approach throughout the entire life cycle is indispensable for efficient administration of applications.

Holistic View of the Solution

In increasingly powerful—and thus more complex—system landscapes, business processes usually do not run on a single software component. To be able to provide complete support for the business process, it is therefore necessary to take all the involved components into account. In addition to the individual component activities, the mutual dependencies and the interfaces between components are also particularly important.

Openness

The complexity mentioned above applies not only to SAP, but to other suppliers as well. SAP's customers also use other vendors' applications. Software with additional tasks that are not covered by SAP solutions, as well as SAP's competitors' products, is partly integrated into the handling of business process. To enable care of the customer's solution from beginning to end, non-SAP products also have to be taken into account. This makes it possible to prevent delays in determining the root cause and to correct problems quickly. SAP Solution Manager makes it possible to integrate such components.

Governance

SAP Solution Manager lets you schedule pending tasks, to orchestrate existing tools and the resulting documentation. To this end, it offers a central platform for governing IT processes, one which plans, controls, and monitors the execution of the activities.

Transparency

The transparency of measures taken is of particular interest where compliance is involved. So is transparent documentation, which is vital to making the right decisions. Accordingly, all the necessary information is collected and made available centrally in SAP Solution Manager.

It is SAP's goal to simplify SAP solutions as much as possible for our customers and to enable efficient support through SAP services. SAP Solution Manager pursues both of these aims. In the tradition of the services for Accelerated SAP (ASAP), which were offered to customers at no additional fee, SAP Solution Manager is available as a central platform to SAP customers and partners free of charge.

3 CobiT Domain: Plan and Organize

The *Plan and Organize* (PO) domain focuses on strategies and tactics for the optimum deployment of IT to fulfill the business requirements. The strategic vision has to be planned, published, and organized. A suitable IT infrastructure and organization are essential to achieving the business aims. Table 3.1 shows the processes associated with this domain and their relation to SAP IT Service & Application Management (ITSAM).

CobiT			ITSAM Process
Do-main	Pro-cess	Control	
PO	1	Define a strategic IT plan	Integration processes
PO	2	Define the information architecture	Integration processes
PO	3	Determine techno-logical direction	Integration processes
PO	4	Define the IT pro-cesses, organization and relationships	Service support and service delivery

CobiT			ITSAM Process
Domain	Process	Control	
PO	5	Manage the IT investment	Financial management for IT services
PO	6	Communicate management aims and direction	
PO	7	Manage IT human resources	Capacity management
PO	8	Manage quality	SAP ITSAM
PO	9	Assess and manage IT risks	Service level management, availability management, IT service continuity management
PO	10	Manage projects	Application management

Table 3.1 Overview of the CobiT Processes in PO and Their Relationship to SAP ITSAM

3.1 PO1: Defining a Strategic IT Plan

To use the IT resources in line with the defined business strategy and its priorities, it is essential to define a strategic IT plan that identifies the components and other resources needed to implement the business strategy. It is important to ensure that all the important decision makers from IT and the business areas understand and evaluate the value potential and the technical limitations of IT solutions. The results are mapped to a project portfolio that covers items such as the content of the project, the most important project steps, and their scheduling, as well as the objectives. The portfolio is used to draft the strategic and tactical IT plans. The speed and flexibility of the IT reaction to business requirements are decisive factors in the organization's competitiveness. Accordingly, IT planning requires permanent portfolio management in the company, and should be treated as an annual (or even one-off) procedure.

Tools

SAP xApp Resource and Portfolio Management

Implementing standard SAP applications in SAP ERP, the Business Information Warehouse, and Strategic Enterprise Management enable you to map a business-based IT management structure. Project portfolio management plays a key role here. The SAP xApp Resource and Portfolio Management (SAP xRPM) solution, which provides a reliable inventory of the entire IT portfolio, can be used as a starter package for SAP's project system.Project proposals can be drawn up, assessed, and assigned priorities. A risk-and-benefit assessment enables you to quickly select the right ideas from the many available. You can identify and implement possible synergy effects from different IT projects more easily. Implementation is supported by cross-project controlling of dates, budgets, and resources, which makes use of the integration with the SAP Human Resources and Accounting solutions. Standardized reports enable you to assess the project's status.

cProjects

SAP xRPM is linked seamlessly with cProjects as a tool for operational project management. You can also merge information from other project management systems and from MS Project. This means that the entire project portfolio is always evident and available. External projects carried out by partners can also be linked. You can access an overview of the entire IT portfolio—in other words a management report based on key figures—in a dedicated dashboard.

Services

It is no longer possible to implement enterprisewide, value-added process chains without IT. SAP's consulting services assist you in developing the appropriate IT strategy for your corporate strategy. The result is a complete view of the future application environment and its technical architecture. Possible scenarios and implementation steps for the application landscape and its architecture are identified.

Enterprise Service-Oriented Business Strategy

The Enterprise Service-Oriented Business Strategy service supports the definition of an integrative Enterprise Service-Oriented Architecture (Enterprise SOA) business strategy that merges the company's business and technological requirements. A framework of individual recommendations then enables you to control the business-specific version of the Enterprise SOA over the long term and across the company.

SAP Solution Business Value Assessment

SAP Solution Business Value Assessment service backs up IT decisions with business facts. This service is used to assess the commercial use of SAP solutions to a company. The results help you to make IT decisions and monitor projects.

SAP IT Strategy Development

The aim of the SAP IT Strategy Development service is to optimize IT support for business processes and to control them in a manner focused on IT value and the markets. This service harmonizes the business goals and the IT strategy, and promotes the flexibility of the IT landscape.

Empowering

Enterprise Architects

SAP Education provides a training course for enterprise architects. This course introduces the tools for planning a company's future IT landscape using corporate objectives and priorities, and teaches how a company's existing IT landscape can be used to implement a developed plan.

3.2 PO2: Defining the Information Architecture

The information architecture forms the basis on which all the necessary information of a financial or technical nature is made available. The information architecture broadly defines which modules are linked to one another. Which technical systems are used to manage and prepare information? Which data is exchanged and how, and how is it linked to create the flow of information? Having the right information at the right time can have a decisive impact on the business, which means the quality of this CobiT process also supports the quality of management decisions. The information has to be trustworthy and must only be accessible to authorized persons.

Tools

SAP NetWeaver

The basics are grounded in SAP NetWeaver's service-oriented architecture, which links, combines, and reconciles people, information and business processes optimally (see Figure 3.1). In the Information Integration layer, SAP provides three essential solutions that customers can use to build information systems.

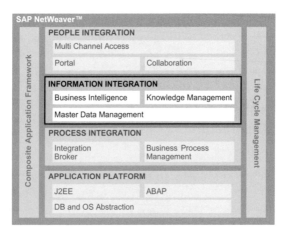

Figure 3.1 SAP NetWeaver Architecture

Business Intelligence

SAP NetWeaver Business Intelligence (BI) enables you to analyze, prepare, and distribute information quickly. The technical foundation consists of a Business Information Warehouse system, in which you can merge and integrate any data from the system landscape. You can even use current data to create forecasts of future trends of key performance indicators (KPIs).

Knowledge Management

Knowledge Management (KM) supports the administration of a knowledge database. It provides a central entry point for access to distributed document management, including a repository. In addition, you can also version and evaluate documents, and connect them with a workflow. An authorization concept allows you to limit access to the documents stored in the system and the information contained therein. Powerful search functions such as text mining and automatic classification simplify finding information.

Master Data Management

Master Data Management (MDM) is used to manage and consolidate master data centrally. As a result, all applications can access a shared, central data pool. MDM can help avoid redundancies and inconsistencies in the master data.

SAP Solution Manager

As part of SAP Solution Manager, SAP supplies preconfigured information architectures and an evaluation option in the Solution Monitoring area that are specially designed for ITSAM requirements.

The functions in SAP Solution Manager can be differentiated according to the SAP lifecycle.

The tasks of the build phase are reflected in the SAP Solution Manager implementation area. This area maps the design phase from the IT Infrastructure Library (ITIL) perspective.

The new business-process platform provides tools (such as the Solution Directory and E-Learning Management) for the deploy phase.

The tools supporting the ITIL operate and optimize phases, however, are located in the SAP Solution Manager's operations area:

▶ **Solution Directory**
The Solution Directory in SAP Solution Manager is the central repository for both phases. Metadata for the business processes and for the technical systems, as well as their interconnections, is listed here. The data in the Solution Directory can easily be used to define business process monitoring, technical monitoring, or service-level reporting, to name just a few.

▶ **EarlyWatch Report**
SAP Solution Manager supports both technical and business-process views of the system landscape. Preconfigured monitors are provided. In the standard system, you can create EarlyWatch reports for each technical system at regular intervals. These reports supply measured tech-

nical values for rating the quality of the ITSAM), which you can then integrate into service level reporting.

▶ **System Landscape Maintenance**
In this process, the SAP Solution Manager uses not only the monitoring tools to procure information, but also the System Landscape Directory (SLD) as a source of information. The SLD contains information about the configuration of components and their relations, such as software releases and support packages used and versions of programs and interfaces. It is an important component in the concept of the Configuration Management Database.

Evaluations over longer periods of time are possible if you transfer the data from the service reports (EarlyWatch Alert) to the Business Information Warehouse integrated in the SAP Solution Manager. The transfer is predefined; you only have to activate it. The powerful BI tools come into their own in the Business Information Warehouse, which also includes graphical formatting.

SAP NetWeaver Security

Security is a subject of fundamental importance to all information architectures. SAP NetWeaver Security addresses a broad range of topics, including user access (e.g., identity and authorization, single sign-on, and user management), application security (e.g., roles and authorization, data security, audits), and secure cooperation (e.g., identity federation in inter-company scenarios, message-level security, trust management).

SAP GRC Access Control

The applications in SAP GRC Access Control enable automatic checks of all access authorizations for possible violations of segregation of duties. The results of this assessment risk analysis are made available as management reports. SAP GRC Access Control also guides managers through the remediation of the violations identified. They can be remedied by removing conflicting access authorizations and separating conflicting business functions between people. In certain cases (such as in small organizations), it may not be possible to distribute the tasks to different persons. In such cases, the compensating or mitigating controls in the SAP GRC Access Control applications help you to introduce additional control steps (such as reports) and responsible persons (known as monitors). This helps to prevent violations of the guidelines and laws on the segregation of duties (such as the Sarbanes-Oxley Act). The relevant reports on mitigating controls are available for auditors.

Services

Premium Engagements

At this point we would like to draw attention to the premium engagements (see Figure 3.2). Premium engagements are provided in addition to SAP's standard support in the form of SAP Safeguarding, SAP MaxAttention, or SAP Premium Support. With these products, SAP supports you in carrying out critical projects or offers you a partnership over the specific period in which your company plans to make critical changes. A standard component of the premium engagements is a number of Solution Management Optimization (SMO) services, which are described when we discuss the relevant CobiT controls in this pocket guide.

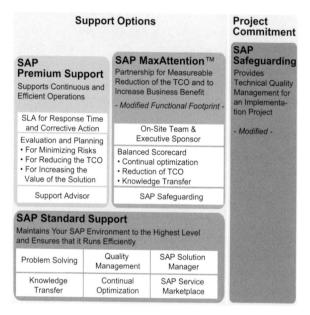

Figure 3.2 Premium Engagements Overview

SAP Solution Manager Roadmap

The service SAP Solution Manager Roadmap offers Premium Engagement customers systematic guidance towards implementing SAP Solution Manager. It also provides information about possible scenarios and examples of alternatives or integrated use of products from other providers that may be relevant to your company.

Empowering

SAP provides training courses and certification for SAP Solution Manager. To support the implementation phase, these courses explore the functions of the roadmap and the blueprint. Another area of focus is the use of the SAP Solution Manager in the operations phase, when the delivery of SAP services, Solution Monitoring, and Service Desk functions comes into effect. SAP also offers a training course on the technical installation of SAP Solution Manager.

3.3 PO3: Determining the Technological Direction

An IT architecture committee is charged with defining a unique, stringent technological direction for the company. To enable the creation of a technological infrastructure plan, experts from the company's core business areas and experts from planning have to meet and formulate their expectations of the products, services, and operating mechanisms. To this end, the task of the technology experts is to classify the relevant technological components and plan the infrastructure accordingly. The plans for the technical infrastructure should also take future trends and regulations into account. One fundamental task of the committee is to determine technical standards, such as the operating or database system strategy, interfaces, data-transfer techniques, and security. These standards should be determined based on their relevance to the business, to risks, and to compliance with external guidelines.

Services

Security Strategy Concept

The service *Security Strategy Concept* evaluates the security risks of the technology being used. Both the security strategy and security concept are investigated. In the first step, the current status is recorded. This as-is analysis includes the risk-management process, the implementation of technical company guidelines, the SAP authorization concept, the implementation of the SAP security concept, and compliance with legal requirements. In a second step, the action that needs to be taken is shown on the basis of the as-is analysis. If desired, a return on security investment can be calculated for the recommended measures. In the third and final step, the sequence and the time frame for the suggested actions are summarized in a master plan.

SAP NetWeaver Value Assessment

The *NetWeaver Value Assessment* service identifies the business-specific advantages that can be achieved by using NetWeaver components as the technological platform. The result is a list of the possible uses of the individual components: Business Intelligence, Exchange Infrastructure, and Master Data Management.

3.4 PO4: Defining the IT Processes, Organization, and Relationships

In an IT organization, all the requirements related to staff, specialized knowledge, functions, liability, authorizations, roles, and responsibilities must be defined, along with the monitoring of these specifications. The basis for this definition is an IT process model that describes all the work steps for creating IT solutions and IT services. ITIL provides a suitable framework here, based on suggestions tried and tested in the real world. ITIL has been extended for SAP solutions to include certain specific processes, roles, and tools for ITSAM. A decisive factor in an organization's success is the definition and implementation of IT quality assurance. In addition to the process description, the use of suitable tools is also important.

The basic prerequisite here is compliance with all regulations, whether specific to the business or required by law. It is therefore essential to clearly regulate who in the company is responsible for risk management, for security, and for compliance with the regulations, as well as specifically for the IT organization. There should be detailed specifications of which persons execute which functions in the organization. You should avoid bundling tasks in a way that could pose security risk. For example, an employee who is authorized to of develop new software functions, test them, and transport them to the production environment would represent a security risk.

An essential factor in the structuring of the internal IT processes is a thorough support concept that maps the in-house support processes transparently.

Because all IT solutions are subject to constant change (either because of new technical developments or the legal environment) it is vital to plan and control these changes to the company. ITIL provides Process Change Management for this purpose. It describes exactly how the organizational implementation of changes should occur and which concrete tasks have to be fulfilled.

Tools

mySAP CRM in Shared Service Centers

In addition to its use at the interface between companies and customers, mySAP CRM is now frequently used on the market for shared service centers. Generally speaking, shared service centers provide central access to interactive services for specific parts of companies within corporate groups, such as the human resources area (HR help desk and Employee Interaction Center). The mySAP CRM Interaction Center enables you to integrate interaction channels (telephone, fax, e-mail, web chat, and so on) into the service and support processes within a shared service center. mySAP CRM Interaction Center is also extremely effective for internal IT help desks.

mySAP CRM and ITIL

In the context of ITIL, an IT help desk covers the core processes of "incident and problem management" and also provides integration with other ITIL areas, such as configuration management. Technical configurations can be copied or updated directly from a mySAP ERP system, or from non-SAP systems via the SAP Exchange Infrastructure (SAP XI), and used in configuration management. The IT help desk has been a standard component of the mySAP CRM Interaction Center since the 2004 SAP CRM edition. Additional reporting is available via SAP Business Information Warehouse.

Service Desk

SAP Solution Manager provides a preconfigured solution for constructing a support concept for the company. This solution was optimized with respect to the specific SAP requirements and can be customized. The Service Desk models various support levels, in which messages can be processed and solved efficiently. A major advantage of this solution is the option of forwarding messages from the customer's support organization directly to SAP. This direct access in the support process reduces support costs. This is supported by technical data, which the Service Desk provides automatically when a message is created. A bidirectional interface makes it possible to exchange messages using tools from other suppliers that are deployed at the company. This makes it possible to create an integrated support concept in heterogeneous system landscapes.

You can use the Service Desk to map your support organization in the system and define the following scenarios.

▶ An enterprise with a support organization

▶ Multiple company segments in an enterprise with one shared support organization

▶ A service provider that services multiple companies

Change Request Management

Change Request Management in the SAP Solution Manager provides a preconfigured process that is aimed at ITIL Change Management and can be customized. The process covers every step from the original change request, such as a support query, to control and monitoring of the technical transport. All the steps in the process are protected against unauthorized access by the SAP user and roles concept. Comprehensive reporting functions round out the Software Change Management offering.

Providing Services

Another IT process that has to be defined is the provision of services for the IT solution. SAP Solution Manager also provides a platform in the SAP support infrastructure for ordering central services and coordinating their delivery. The advantage of this thorough approach is that service providers have a single point from which to access all the relevant information, such as documentation, business processes, test cases and monitoring information. This information makes service delivery faster and more consistent, because service engineers can work within a standardized structure.

SAP GRC Access Control

The SAP GRC Access Control applications are used to implement the required legal and company-specific policies for proper segregation of duties. If you integrate all the relevant IT systems, you can implement and monitor this across the enterprise. This makes it possible to quickly identify and eliminate access risks in the IT landscape, as well as install preventative controls.

► **Virsa Compliance Calibrator**

The Virsa Compliance Calibrator is the central component of the SAP GRC Access Control applications. The Virsa Compliance Calibrator is used to link in all major ERP systems and to analyze the corresponding user and authorization information. For this purpose, the Virsa Compliance Calibrator has access to one of the most comprehensive rule libraries of predefined "access risks." It enables companies to analyze the access risks in their IT applications, identify critical combinations of business functions in an employee profile, and then remediate the problems. Virsa Compliance Calibrator connects with the SAP ERP systems in real time.

► **Virsa Role Expert**

Virsa Role Expert standardizes and centralizes the design, testing, and maintenance of roles. Even from the first step—role design—the focus is on consistent segregation of duties.

► **Virsa FireFighter for SAP**

Virsa FireFighter for SAP is available for employees in the event of an emergency. Employees can select one of the predefined and pre-assigned "privileged authorizations" (FireFighter IDs) for themselves in special situations. All of an employee's activities are then logged and made available as a management or audit report. As a further security measure, an approval process is then triggered. This addresses the number one audit issue raised by temporary super-user access: how to prevent risks associated with granting employees the most comprehensive super-user authorization (SAP_ALL) in the event of an emergency in an IT organization, given that the activities carried out using this authorization are not monitored.

▶ **Virsa Access Enforcer**

Authorizations change every day as employees are redeployed. New user accounts and access authorizations must be created for new employees, and user accounts and access authorizations must be deleted for departed personnel. The Virsa Access Enforcer supports the analysis of critical authorizations and critical business function combinations for one person. When an authorization is requested, the system simulates the combination of the already assigned authorizations and the additionally requested authorization(s) and provides that information to the managers who can approve access. If violations of segregation of duties are found, the managers are guided through a structured remediation process. This tool helps companies implement effective preventive controls.

SAP GRC Process Control

In many companies, it is taken for granted that internal checks have to be implemented to safeguard the handling of the most important business processes. The supporting IT processes are a component of these checks. SAP GRC Process Control contains best practices for documenting this kind of process risk, as well as internal checks best suited to avoiding these process risks. In addition, SAP GRC Process Control includes the option of ongoing monitoring for internal checks in key SAP processes. These tests take place at periodic intervals specified by the user, either automatically or manually.

Services

CCC Strategy Development

The *CCC Strategy Development* service supports customers in establishing a Customer Competence Center (CCC). One of the results of this service is the definition of the CCC's service portfolio. Potential organizational models are also elaborated and evaluated. The breadth of the organization can range from a central structure to a decentralized structure, such as by regions or business areas. As part of the service, the necessary roles and the required professional background of the personnel to be used are determined.

SAP Discovery Server

Different SAP NetWeaver components and development tools are combined in the *SAP Discovery Server* to execute an application based on an Enterprise Service-Oriented Architecture (Enterprise SOA). The Discovery Server speeds up the (prototypical) implementation of the customer-specific roadmap and thus the realization of business benefits. It makes it easier to access the Enterprise SOA world, reduces the cost of developing your own SOA scenarios and feasibility studies, and demonstrates the use of the SAP NetWeaver platform and the development tools for creating SOA-based applications. All in all, customers can gain SOA development knowledge more quickly. Example scenarios have also been elaborated for the SAP GRC Access Control components.

3.5 PO5: Managing the IT Investment

Once the requirements have been established, the budget available for IT investment has to be managed in line with priorities. To do this, the products used in the IT organization (such as the licenses for the deployed solutions, monitoring tools, and the service desk) are defined and calculated, and a costs, resources, and investment control system is put in place. Once the IT services' prices have been determined, cost management can be established on the basis of activity allocation.

Tools

The processes needed to manage the IT investment can be mapped using standardized SAP ERP, BW, and SEM functions. Strategic planning, financial planning, budgeting, and financial forecasting are realized with SAP Strategic Enterprise Management (SEM). Specific service packages are mapped for the IT services and defined as products, including product costing. An internal transfer price is then mapped on the basis of the cost estimate, and invoiced when the service is purchased. An open interface makes it possible to determine the quantity used, with the help of usage key figures. To plan required quantities adequately, the IT department agrees on service contracts and service plans with its customers. These can also be mapped, managed, and monitored using SAP software.

Services

SAP Consulting provides customer-specific support for IT value management. We recommend prioritizing IT projects on the basis of a cost/benefit analysis. To analyze use, you should include strategic, normative, and operative aspects in the calculation. The strategic benefit analysis evaluates questions such as the time taken for an idea for a new requirement to be launched on the market, the speed of opening new fields of business, and creating competitive advantages. Normative benefit analysis examines technical necessity in the business areas and legal requirements. The simplification and acceleration of processes in the IT organization are evaluated from an operational perspective. Thanks to comprehensive best practices, SAP Consulting can support you in drawing up and implementing a key figure system to establish benefit evaluation and use control.

3.6 PO6: Communicating Management Aims and Direction

Management is responsible for developing an IT Control Framework. The IT Control Framework should ensure that all the relevant laws and guidelines are complied with. The guidelines and procedures that have to be observed should be explained in detail and communicated accordingly. It is important to note that this is not a one-off procedure, but one in which all affected employees and decision makers should be informed and prepared for future requirements based on systematic, targeted information.

Tools

SAP GRC Repository

The SAP GRC Repository can be used as a central store for all regulations, guidelines, and associated risks, as well as controls and audit evidence. This means that all enterprise-wide information about sustainable governance, risk management, and compliance with regulatory requirements is stored in (and can be accessed from) one central location, improving transparency. All relevant status reports and management decisions are also stored centrally in the same location. This centralized storage makes it easier for management and auditors to find the relevant documents. Furthermore, central management helps to identify and abolish redundant controls throughout the organization.

Solution Monitoring

SAP Solution Manager supports you in defining projects and clearly communicating the aims of these projects. But in the operating and optimizing phases, it also offers you the option of monitoring the IT solution and reacting in a timely fashion to violations of the guidelines, thanks to Solution Monitoring.

Change Request Management

To make sure that all changes are harmonized in line with the defined guidelines, you can use Change Request Management to ensure that changes have to be approved by a change manager or change advisory board. Each step, from the request to approvals and from technical implementation to control of the transport to downstream systems, is transparent and reproducible at all times.

3.7 PO7: Managing IT Human Resources

IT processes cannot be professionally implemented without a competent IT staff. One of the core personnel management tasks is recruiting and training staff, while another is processing staff departures. Jobs are granted on the basis of the defined roles, as are changing jobs and altering areas of responsibility. This includes checking the eligibility of employees, suppliers, and customers to carry out critical and/or sensitive tasks in IT, such as maintaining security-related company data. You also need to assess the company's dependence on individual persons and the related risk should these people no longer be available (such as the loss of know-how). If the identified risks are too high, suitable action must be taken.

Tools

mySAP ERP Human Capital Management provides the most modern and comprehensive functions for Human Resources. It supports the areas of talent management, personnel administration, workforce planning, and reporting, for example.

Talent
The area of talent development covers support for recruitment, career management, and succession planning. The talent pool in SAP E-Recruiting combines external and in-

ternal recruitment in a single platform. This improves candidates' career opportunities while giving line managers a greater choice when searching for suitable applicants.

Personnel Administration

Personnel administration covers employee management, from time recording through to payroll accounting and creating legal evaluations.

Workforce Planning

Workforce planning can be used to put together project teams on the basis of employee qualifications and current availability.

Reporting

Reporting can evaluate and analyze current situations in human resources, which clears the path for modern personnel work.

SAP Learning Solution

The SAP Learning Solution merges all the educational processes on a single platform. The SAP Learning Solution covers all the relevant educational processes, makes it possible to control education on the basis of key figures, and is completely integrated into mySAP ERP. In this approach, the solution connects learning and business processes, enabling you to synchronize education management with your business strategy. Educational processes can be mapped as closed and linked to personnel administration, personnel development, organization development, and accounting.

The SAP Learning Solution is a complete solution that provides a learning portal, a learning management system, and a learning content management system:

▶ **Learning Portal**
The SAP Learning Solution can be accessed by every employee, supplier, and partner via an Enterprise Portal, provided that they have the necessary authorization. Employees can access the learning portal via a personal start page at their workplaces. This means that role- and task-specific learning content can be made available to individual employees or to specific groups. The personalized training course can be aimed specifically at individual training requirements, at updating previously obtained qualifications, or at new professional requirements.

▶ **Learning Management System**
The learning management system controls the learning process. It suggests learning units on the basis of information about the learners, tracks learning progress, and coordinates the personal learning process.

▶ **Learning Content Management**
Learning content is stored, managed in, and distributed from Learning Content Management. Tools for making controlled changes to the content are integrated for administrative purposes. This includes version management and protection of content against parallel changes. Because of their respective experience and areas of responsibility, employees have different types of knowledge. The available distribution mechanisms can

be used to target learning content to employees who are really affected and interested.

SAP GRC Access Control

Each change to the makeup of the personnel structure (hires, transfers, and departures) can involve risks to authorization profiles and the associated scope of system use. Virsa Access Control makes it possible to determine whether the relevant segregation of duties was observed for the employees in question. Each individual request to change an authorization can be processed quickly, efficiently, and in harmony with the segregation of duties requirements. All responsible managers receive the information needed to make a decision via workflow. If it is not possible to separate tasks—perhaps because the employee is responsible for the entire process at a small external site, for example—SAP GRC Access Control provides a selection of suitable measures for minimizing the risk. One possibility is a detailed log of security-related activities.

Empowering

The longest stage in a solution's life cycle is the productive phase, which also takes up the largest part of the budget. This phase also often presents great challenges to chief information officers and their teams, as well as increased risks for daily operations.

SAP provides special training courses and certification for employees in Customer Competence Centers and other highly specialized IT workers, such as solution architects and application/SAP NetWeaver managers. The courses include conventional classroom training and e-learning solutions.

3.8 PO8: Managing Quality

The basis for this control is a quality-management system in which the quality-assured development and purchasing processes are mapped. Standardized IT processes are implemented for this purpose (based on ITIL, for example). Suitable quality criteria have to be defined for IT processes at the planning and organization stages. Defining quality criteria alone is not enough, however; quality criteria can only be checked and adjusted if suitable measuring methods have been planned and implemented. Once this is accomplished, improvement measures can be introduced for the affected IT processes and the success of the measures can be measured.

Tools

Service Level Reporting

Service Level Reporting in SAP Solution Manager is an important tool for service outsourcing. In Service Level Reporting, you can use the data from EarlyWatch Alerts (EWA) and add any data from the monitoring area. You can even assess the data against stored threshold values (ratings). You can collect raw data from the EWA according to customer-specific requirements and adjust assessments. EWA reports from multiple systems can be grouped into a single report. These monitoring and reporting functions make it significantly easier to monitor compliance with service level agreements (SLAs). The true challenge here is identifying the practical items for your business process from the wide range of possibilities.

Service Desk

The Service Desk automatically provides technical data in the event of an incident. This makes it possible to improve the quality of the support processes. It also automatically forwards the incident to the relevant support team, which makes it possible to eliminate malfunctions faster.

Change Request Management

Change Request Management uses the structure of the maintenance cycle to ensure that all developers adhere to the change management process defined by the company. For example, it can ensure that only changes that have previously been approved can actually be implemented. From a quality perspective, it is more important that transports arising from changes can only be imported into the production environment once the correction has been successfully tested.

Test Management

SAP Solution Manager provides a comprehensive portfolio for testing solutions developed. This portfolio covers everything from creating test plans and assigning testers through to the status analysis of the tests. It is also possible to integrate third-party tools. Test management offers the option of managing and executing tests along business-process lines, making them operational across systems and controllable from a central point. Test cases are stored at the relevant business processes or process steps. Testers work in the same structure as project employees who carry out the configuration. This guarantees a seamless transfer between the project phases and the effective transfer of knowledge.

SAP GRC Process Control

SAP GRC Process Control identifies risks in businesses processes supported by IT. A quality-control review of business processes can establish whether they are being processed in line with company guidelines. SAP GRC Process Control can deploy automated checkpoints into business processes, to report on compliance with company policy. In order to produce the monthly or annual financial statement, for example, the reports and statement programs must be scheduled and run in a rigidly kept sequence. The infrastructure and support must be constructed from the IT perspective so that they fulfill the performance and data consistency requirements, particularly when large data volumes are involved.

mySAP PLM

mySAP Product Lifecycle Management (mySAP PLM) provides a central point of access to quality management, thanks to the global exchange and checking of relevant information. The solution supports all quality management processes in a company. Its use of role concepts makes it possible to implement a broad range of tasks efficiently and quickly, and lets all employees access the company's current quality guidelines.

3.9 PO9: Assessing and Managing IT Risks

Business processes today are primarily supported by IT. At the same time, functioning IT processes are often a key prerequisite for handling the business processes. For this reason, IT breakdowns and inconsistent data generally lead to business problems. It is therefore essential that you assess and deduce your business risks for effective IT risk management. You need to check whether IT services can support the necessary business processes in a controllable and safe manner, and whether this can be done quickly enough. Taking the business processes as a base, risks are identified and assessed, and suitable improvement measures are introduced where applicable. Since this is not a one-time procedure, continuous improvement is promoted in the form of a risk action plan.

From the perspective of IT operations, the following aspects should be considered to measure the quality of the IT services and to safeguard them in a sustained manner:

▶ **Service Level Management**
   Service Level Management is not only for quality management; it also helps to identify and reduce risks. Suitable measured values and details of their history can help you know if and when critical states are reached. In this way, incidents can be avoided. The better the key figures are adjusted to the important business processes, the more the measurements can help avoid risk. Ideally, compliance with the defined key figures guarantees stable, high-performance, controlled and avail-

able operation of the business processes. Important key figures from the business processes are therefore often transferred to the technical requirements and key figures. When defining key figures, you should always take into account availability, performance, reaction and solution times, and escalation routes.

► **Availability Management**
The IT services should be available when users and the corresponding business processes need them. From a user's point of view, availability is always measured against the readiness and functional efficiency of the applications running in the business processes. The availability of the IT services is vitally important, but in certain circumstances that may not be enough to ensure the necessary functional efficiency of the business processes. In a project, there has to be a shared understanding of availability. The capacities of the infrastructure are optimized as part of availability management. Requirements are derived by answering the following questions:

- ► What is the required minimum duration of availability between two breakdowns?

- ► What is the maximum downtime that can be tolerated?

- ► How is the resistance between incidents and their associated breakdown security assessed?

- ► Can applications be maintained only by the developers themselves, or can application support be carried out by third parties?

- ▶ Is it possible to maintain the application such that changes can be implemented while the applications are in operation?

▶ **Continuity Management**
Continuity Management is responsible for drawing up, developing, and implementing disaster strategies. The aim here is to ensure that there is an agreed-upon IT service level if business operations are interrupted. The effort, expense, and the usefulness of these actions are assessed. After all, it only makes sense to invest in availability and continuity management if they cost less than the breakdowns.

Tools

SAP Solution Manager

One of the main functions of SAP Solution Manager is as the SAP tool that maps the Service Desk function and the processes for reacting to and solving incidents and problems. Various analysis, monitoring, and maintenance tools are integrated into SAP NetWeaver, and these serve to prevent technical breakdowns and provide assistance should they occur.

SAP GRC Access Control Application

Unclear authorization concepts and heterogeneous systems encourage fraud, identity abuse, and the theft and manipulation of data. The SAP GRC Access Control Application helps you to prevent unauthorized access. Its around-the-clock monitoring functions and preventive control mechanisms, as well as immediate risk assessments, help ensure that legal requirements and guidelines are complied with.

SAP GRC Process Control

In future SAP GRC Process Control will be used to implement checkpoints or measuring points for both business processes and IT processes. You can set up automatic checks for the sales process, for example, starting with receiving customer orders and ending with the incoming payment. These checks exclude as far as possible human error or deliberate manipulation. In this case, the checks are implemented to expose incomplete revenue postings and deliveries. To monitor the quality of the IT processes, SAP and Cisco jointly integrated IT infrastructure checks into the GRC Process Control for data transfer in the network. This makes it possible to automatically identify problems such as loss of data or changes to the configuration.

Services

Technical Risk Management for the Implementation Project

SAP Safeguarding enables you to identify risks in implementation projects. The focus here is on recognizing the technical requirements that have to be complied with to ensure that the core business processes run smoothly. The system uses this technical risk analysis as the basis for suggesting improvement measures.

Business Continuity Management

SAP supports you in drawing up disaster plans, including developing a strategy to minimize the severity of the disaster. The disaster plan also takes industry-specific and legal requirements into account.

3.10 PO10: Managing Projects

A key part of successful project management is getting all the necessary people responsible for the business involved. This ensures that the project is approved and supported at the management level. The basis for succeeding with a project is adequate planning, including the necessary resources. Each project involves planning risk and quality management in the PO10 control. It is important not to forget to specify criteria for when a project can be considered complete, and to define a transfer plan for transferring a project to operations.

It is therefore important to structure the project management transparently, to carry it out professionally, to clearly define the scope of the project, and to be in a position to eliminate impending bottlenecks quickly and efficiently. If you achieve this, you can protect your company's investment, use resources in a targeted manner, set priorities, and ensure clear communication between all those involved in the project.

Tools

Project Management in SAP Solution Manager

SAP Solution Manager supports the administration and definition of projects and project plans. You can define project goals and the scope of the project. In addition to this, you can document the project plan, specify the duration and the project standard, and allocate employees to the project. SAP Solution Manager involves more than simply planning projects. It also allows you to develop requirements for the system landscape needed for the project. SAP Solution Manager is a consequent next step to the proven ASAP (Accelerated SAP) methodology.

Roadmaps

Roadmaps provide a methodical framework for SAP projects. They provide a structured representation of the results and activities, as well as of the necessary or recommended tools, services, and other methodical processes, which you can use to successfully complete your project. The procedures, activities, and results that you will need to support a software project are demonstrated at each phase of the project. This includes implementation accelerators such as templates and best practices, which provide additional added value to the project work.

Business Blueprint

In the Business Blueprint, you define the scope of the project in relation to the business processes. SAP provides business content in the Business Process Repository (BPR). You can use this content to accelerate implementation projects with the help of preconfigured business processes. At the end of the Business Blueprint phase, the scope is summarized in a Business Blueprint document and the structure is transferred for configuration.

Configuration
During the configuration phase, all the relevant information from the Business Blueprint (such as documentation) is made available to the project team in the process structure in SAP Solution Manager. The systems are stored in the SAP Solution Manager system landscape and are linked via Remote Function Call (RFC) connections, making it possible to configure these systems directly from a central point.

Test Management
The conclusion of the configuration phase is the testing phase, which can be carried out using test management in SAP Solution Manager. Test cases can be stored for the business processes and grouped together into test packages and test plans. Roadmaps are available to provide a methodical approach. They provide detailed instructions on project tasks in the test phase, making it easer to implement projects successfully. The test plan makes it possible to plan the test activities in the project clearly and transparently. You can use your own reporting to assess the status of the test.

Cutover in Operations
The business process structure from the configuration phase is transferred to operations in the cutover. In the SAP Solution Manager, all the relevant information is transferred

to the Solution Directory, giving you central access to all the information, such as the documentation, test cases, and configuration objects. In addition to this, you can use E-Learning Management to create Learning Maps in the SAP Solution Manager. You can reuse objects from the project structure in these learning maps.

cProjects

In addition to the established SAP Solution Manager project-management functions, cProjects enables you to create a web-based, higher-level project plan for your SAP Solution Manager projects. This plan supports you in checking compliance with project methodologies and makes the transition between project phases easier, thanks to transfer meetings and milestones.

4 CobiT Domain: Acquire and Implement

The CobiT *Acquire and Implement* (AI) domain encompasses the controls that are important for acquisition, implementation, and introduction of software products. This includes the processes for the acquisition and maintenance of the infrastructure (shown in Table 4.1) as well as IT resources required for the software.

CobiT			ITSAM Process
Do-main	Pro-cess	Control	
AI	1	Identify automated solutions	Application Management, Integration Processes
AI	2	Acquire and maintain application software	Release Management, Change Management
AI	3	Acquire and maintain technology infrastructure	Release Management, Change Management, Integration Processes
AI	4	Enable operation and use	Operations, Integration Processes

CobiT			ITSAM Process
Do-main	Pro-cess	Control	
AI	5	Procure IT resources	Release Management, Capacity Management, Financial Management for IT Services, Integration Processes
AI	6	Manage changes	Change Management
AI	7	Install and accredit solutions and changes	Release Management

Table 4.1 Overview of the CobiT Processes in AI and Their Relationship to SAP ITSAM

4.1 AI1: Identifying Automated Solutions

A feasibility study should be conducted before acquiring applications or developing solutions. Alternative solutions should be examined during the feasibility study to see whether they can be implemented and operated in a way that fulfils business requirements. This involves an analysis of commercial and technological functions. Risk analysis and cost effectiveness are other criteria used to reach a final decision. The risk analysis is used to examine hazards relating to data integration, security, availability, data protection, and adherence to regulations and legal directives. The evaluation of these criteria is used as a basis for the decision whether to purchase an application or to develop an enterprise-specific solution (the make-or-buy decision).

Tools

SAP Solution Maps

SAP uses Solution Maps to describe the functions of SAP software. The business operations typical of the industry involved are used as a reference structure. Figure 4.1 shows an example of a Solution Map. You can branch to the detailed view by choosing the solution elements you require. You can view all Solution Maps under: *http://www.sap.com/solutions/businessmaps*.

Services

SAP Value Assessment

SAP Value Assessment supports you by determining the value potential that is hidden in an investment in information technology. A comparison of existing and expected cost-efficiency structures shows the possible return on investment (ROI). This enables a company to measure the potential added-value of a project before it has even begun.

IT Sourcing Strategy

As part of its *IT Sourcing Strategy* service, SAP analyzes the IT value chain in a company. Later, SAP can provide decision support to help the company choose which services to provide for itself and which services must be purchased.

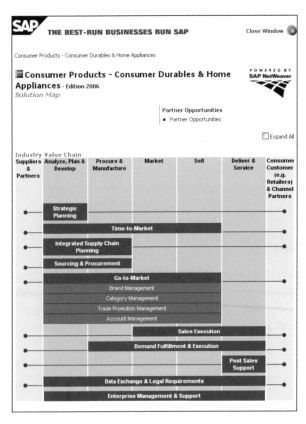

Figure 4.1 Solution Map for the Consumer Products Industry

4.2 AI2: Acquiring and Maintaining Application Software

The available software solutions must support the business operation requirements. The detail design phase, in which a comprehensive target concept is drawn up, follows the rough design phase, which takes into account the functional requirements and integration into the existing IT environment. The target concept also covers the issues of reproducibility, transparency, and acceptability by supervisory bodies. The target concept also defines the security and availability requirements of the intended solution. The business controls must be mapped correctly in the application. In particular, the requirements for authorizations, access controls, and data backup must be taken into account. The risks that are inherent in handling confidential business data are evaluated. You must then determine how these risks can be minimized or controlled to an acceptable extent, depending on the level of risk and the importance of the operation involved.

Test procedures are conducted in the final configuration and implementation phase. There is not only potential for problems in terms of function, but also in the areas of performance, interfaces to existing applications, and creating documentation and the participant handbook.

The same test procedures should be prepared and conducted even when the software involved is not a new acquisition but "only" a major functional enhancement as part of an upgrade.

You must ensure that the implemented software corresponds to the original design criteria. An acceptance process involving the business process owners makes certain that the solution is appropriate in terms of the business, functional, and technical requirements. You should make sure that all legal and contractual requirements have been identified and fulfilled. A quality-management process provides the methodical basis for the planning and implementation of the intermediate acceptance processes that accompany the development. Quality management involves the testing, inspection and trial runs of complete business scenarios.

All changes to the originally specified requirements are processed in the Change Management process, which must be established during commissioning and defines the procedure for approving changes and their implementation once they have been approved. Examples of changes include the rectification of errors, or functional improvements such as performance optimization or adaptation to new process requirements. All changes are subject to the Change Management process, which ensures that IT services essential for business operations continue to fulfill the quality criteria defined in the Service Level Management after changes have been made, and therefore remain satisfactory for the users.

Tools

SAP GRC Access Control

The SAP GRC Access Control applications clean up the existing user access and authorizations with respect to proper segregation of duties. This involves removal of unnecessary, conflict-triggering authorizations. If this is not possible, you will need to introduce corresponding mitigating or compensating controls that encompass compensating measures, such as additional reporting and monitoring steps. This application makes it possible, for example, to help guarantee process reliability by preventing the same person from ordering, accepting, and paying for software in one procurement process.

Business Blueprint

The business processes to be mapped can be documented in SAP Solution Manager. All relevant business scenarios, business processes, and process steps are given a hierarchical structure. The project documentation can also be created by applying the hierarchical structure of the business scenarios. Transactions, documentation, test cases, and configuration items, for example, can be assigned to every structural element of this hierarchy (scenario, process, process step). It can also include processes that do not run in SAP systems, but instead run in non-SAP components in the system landscape. This defines how the business processes are to run in the IT solution. SAP provides preconfigured data in the Business Process Repository along with thoroughly documented content that can be adapted to the customer's requirements. As a result, processes do not have to be defined completely from scratch, but instead can be configured quickly using standard templates.

Test Workbench

The Test Workbench that is included in SAP Solution Manager contains the Test Organizer and tools for test automation. The business-process structure is also used to administer test cases in SAP Solution Manager. The Test Organizer supports the administration of tests including planning, reporting, and problem tracking. The transactions that were assigned to process steps in the Business Blueprint are inserted in test plans during test-plan generation. They can be processed as function tests to test the individual transactions. The Extended Computer Aided Test Tool (eCATT) enables companies to conduct automated tests in a complete IT solution landscape.

SAP Test Data Migration Server (TDMS)

SAP Test Data Migration Server (TDMS) is a data extraction tool that supplies the development, test, quality assurance, and training systems with business data from the SAP production system.

Change Request Management

The Change Request Management in SAP Solution Manager is the tool for the central administration, documentation, and evaluation of changes. Release Management and Change Management are closely linked to each other. In the broadest sense, a release upgrade is also a change. Working on this assumption, you can administer release upgrades as part of an upgrade project with the aid of Change Request Management in SAP Solution Manager. The Change Request Management maps the entire change-management process, from the request to commissioning in the live system. In this scenario, the maintenance processes provide the option of using faster and partially automated maintenance measures, such as identifying Support Packages or SAP Notes and implementing them with Change Request Management.

Support Packages and Support Package Stacks

Support Packages provide groups of corrections for serious software errors in SAP systems. The corrections are collated periodically in Support Packages and made available at the SAP Service Marketplace (*http://www.service.sap.com*). Since 2003, Support Package Stacks have been used to provide an optimized process for importing maintenance updates. They group together all relevant Support Packages for a product; i. e., all software components, kernels, etc. This simplifies the maintenance process, because it is no longer necessary to search for individual Support Packages for software components, as they can be found in a convenient, compatible collection.

Maintenance Optimizer

Using this infrastructure as a base, SAP Solution Manager and the Maintenance Optimizer will act as a central platform for all maintenance measures in effect from January 2007 on. Maintenance measures can also be obtained from the SAP Service Marketplace during a transition period until

April 2007. From April 2007 onwards, SAP Solution Manager will be the sole source for maintenance updates for the mySAP Business Suite and all applications that are based on SAP NetWeaver 2004s. The platform can also be used for maintenance updates for older versions of SAP software components.

Some of the benefits of the Maintenance Optimizer for the maintenance of SAP applications are as follows:

▶ Standardized, end-to-end processes for the administration and maintenance of the entire SAP landscape

▶ Single point of access for planning and implementing all maintenance activities

▶ Primary source for all Support Packages that are provided under the terms of a maintenance contract

Services

Feasibility Check of the Business Blueprint
The *Technical Integration Check* (TIC) from the SAP Safeguarding service range supports customers by checking technical feasibility (Check of Blueprint) and implementing customer requirements in the suggested solution. This approach helps highlight potential risks.

SAP Test Management
SAP consulting services provide support in the design and execution of functional tests and the performance of load and stress tests.

Authorization Concept for SAP

The service *Authorization Concept for SAP* provides support in the planning, design, implementation, acceptance, and go-live of SAP-relevant authorization profiles.

SAP's Maintenance Strategy

In 2005, SAP took considerable measures to simplify its maintenance strategy. The strategy fixes the duration and conditions of maintenance, thereby facilitating high levels of planning reliability for customers. SAP NetWeaver, the applications from the mySAP Business Suite range, and SAP industry solutions use a 5-1-2 maintenance strategy:

▶ *Mainstream Maintenance* provides five years of maintenance for the standard maintenance fee.

▶ *Extended Maintenance* is then available for a period of one year with an additional fee of 2 %.

▶ If the customer continues to operate releases once this sixth year has elapsed, SAP continues to offer *Extended Maintenance* for an additional fee of 4 % per year.

In line with SAP's motto "support never ends," support services are available to customers even when the Mainstream Maintenance and Extended Maintenance phases have ended for their releases. This phase, which extends maintenance according to customer requirements, is called Customer-Specific Maintenance.

Empowering

SAP Product Documentation

Information on covering requirements in standard functions of SAP software is available in the SAP product documentation. This information can be found at the SAP Help Portal (*http://help.sap.com*).

4.3 AI3: Acquiring and Maintaining Technology Infrastructure

This process relates to the acquisition, maintenance, and securing of infrastructures. It must comply with the agreed technology strategies, development guides, and testing techniques.

The acquisition of fixed assets must be conducted transparently and with adherence to legal requirements in mind. Availability of services that are necessary for maintaining the infrastructure must also be considered.

You must evaluate which systems are required to run business processes, in order to estimate the quality of the technical infrastructure. Once this has been established, availability of the technical infrastructure must be ensured and maintenance processes to ensure continuous improvement defined.

Tools

SAP Service and Asset Management

SAP Service and Asset Management provides the necessary tools for increasing revenues and margins for services and for turning the service into a competitive advantage. SAP Service and Asset Management helps to reduce maintenance and service costs, to increase the reliability and availability of the systems, and to improve productivity and overall return on assets.

The solution also helps ensure that the regulatory requirements of supervisory authorities such as the Food and Drug Administration (FDA) and work safety administration (OSHA) are fulfilled, and directives such as the Sarbanes-Oxley Act are adhered to. Furthermore, all those involved in service and infrastructure maintenance processes (employees, partners, customers, and so on) all should have a common, integrated view of all service activities. In this approach, SAP Service and Asset Management supports adherence to Service Level Agreements, for example, as well as functions such as customer services, internal maintenance, and repairs or spare-parts management (including execution and planning).

SAP Business Maps

SAP Business Maps are graphical overview diagrams of business operations. They can be used as orientation aids in the planning and implementation of a consistent, integrated, and comprehensive IT solution. SAP Business Maps focus on industry-specific processes and help to evaluate and implement innovative software technology. SAP Business Maps can also be used to answer questions relating to infrastructure and technology. The Application Maps clearly depict infrastructure and portfolio services, such as the setup of an IT support organization. Figure 4.2 shows an example of such a Solution Map for an IT support organization.

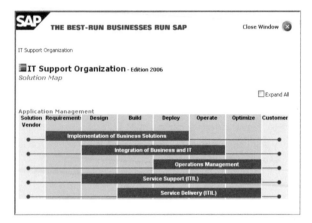

Figure 4.2 Solution Map IT Support Organization on www.sap.com/solutions/businessmaps

Business Process Repository

The Business Process Repository provides a structured directory of business operations. All scenarios and processes are centrally available and can be used as a point of departure for a company-specific modeling of business processes. The scenarios are grouped according to area and content and contain information about the technical components necessary to implement the business concepts.

System Landscape

System landscape maintenance (transaction SMSY) in SAP Solution Manager records all systems relevant to the solution and their roles in the system landscape; e.g., development system, test system, or production system. The System Landscape Directory can be used as a source for the system landscape in SAP Solution Manager.

Solution Manager Diagnostics

Solution Manager Diagnostics supports root-cause analysis for system components that are implemented in ABAP, Java, or C(++), or that run on the Microsoft .NET framework. Solution Manager Diagnostics offers standard functions for:

▶ Performance and resource metrics

▶ Access to technical configuration

▶ Logs and dumps (program terminations)

▶ Traces

▶ Reproducing software changes (code), configurations, or content

Change Request Management

Changes to the hardware, databases, or the programs themselves are part of the operation of an IT solution. Potential risks are inherent in every change, given that essential business transactions can be impaired or interrupted. Accordingly, it is important to analyze and plan for all components in both a reactive and proactive manner, especially in highly integrated solution landscapes. To facilitate this, SAP provides the corresponding services, best practices, and functions in the area of Change Request Management in SAP Solution Manager.

Test Management

As described in Section 4.2, the Test Workbench included in SAP Solution Manager contains the Test Organizer and tools for test automation. The test cases are stored centrally in the Solution Directory of SAP Solution Manager and can be used to test correct procedure after existing business processes are changed.

Test Data Migration Server and Mercury Loadrunner

The Test Data Migration Servers is used to read out real data from production systems selectively and make this data available as test data in development and test system environments. To test the reliability and performance of technical infrastructure and safeguard them in this manner, Solution Manger Diagnostics in SAP Solution Manager also offers the option of conducting load tests with Mercury Loadrunner.

SAP Quick Sizer

SAP provides the SAP Quick Sizer so that you can make the initial definition of the required infrastructure. SAP Quick Sizer is a web-based tool that has been developed in close cooperation between SAP and all of its platform partners to simplify the dimensioning of infrastructure. It is available free of charge. The tool queries the most important key figures and scales of the intended IT solution and business processes and uses them as a basis to estimate the requirements in terms of technical resources. Further information on SAP Quick Sizer can be found at *http://service.sap.com/quicksizer*.

Services

Packaged Service Offering: Technical Risk Assessment
This service provides a comprehensive technical risk analysis. The SAP landscape, including the installed SAP internet scenarios, are checked for security risks using Best Practices, such as the SAP NetWeaver Portal manual and automatic tools such as Watchfire AppScan, ISS Scanner, and others.

Test Management Optimization
The service *Test Management Optimization* offers an evaluation of your current test procedures within two days. The assessment examines the following areas (among others) with regard to optimization potential:

▶ Test organization and embedding in the overall application management

▶ Test standards

▶ Test roles

▶ Test tools

▶ Test automation approaches

▶ Test levels, such as integration testing

The results are compiled in a findings report that makes recommendations for optimizing the above areas, as well as others.

At the end of the assessment, a full-day workshop is held where experts from SAP Test Management Consulting present their testing team and the various SAP testing tools. Particular emphasis is placed on their use in the design of efficient test development and organization.

SAP GoingLive Check

The *SAP GoingLive Check* service usually consists of three separate service sessions, each with a different focus. The Analysis session takes place about six weeks before going live, and involves comparing the expected business volume with the current configuration and the planned hardware resources. Based on the results, a reliable statement can be made as to whether the planned business volume can be handled by the hardware and configuration. Shortly before the actual start of production, the performance of the most important business processes is measured and, if necessary, optimization measures are suggested. About four weeks after going live, the Verification session checks the expected and actual conditions and suggests improvements, in particular to the configuration and performance.

Solution Optimization and Upgrade

The *Solution Optimization and Upgrade* range of services support you in harmonizing the palette of new SAP releases with functional requirements and business objectives. A complete range of services is available, including upgrades, technology, business processes, training, and change and risk management. They also ensure that the IT infrastructure is kept up-to-date in terms of new challenges and innovations.

Certification

By certifying software from other manufactures, SAP guarantees that the software and hardware used in the SAP application environment has been tested by SAP and meets all stability and performance requirements.

4.4 AI4: Enabling Operation and Use

To enable the operation of new IT applications, knowledge of new company processes must be made available. Manuals and documentation of the new applications and technology must be provided and appropriate training made available to end users and IT department personnel, so they can use the applications and infrastructure adequately. Because many projects are carried out by external service providers, it is essential that documentation standards be defined beforehand, to ensure that the documented knowledge can be used efficiently. It is equally important that all information be stored in a central area. This will simplify access and, if necessary (in case of changes, for example), allow you to efficiently update documentation or training materials.

This requires an infrastructure that facilitates the transfer of knowledge, project management that ensures the quality of the materials, and sufficient time for these tasks as defined in Application Management after ITIL in the deploy phase.

Furthermore, a support concept must be drawn up for the operation of a solution that ensures the availability and correct functioning of business processes.

Tools

Document Management in SAP Solution Manager
Project documentation is stored centrally in SAP Solution Manager and transferred to the Solution Directory when the solution begins operating. Standardized templates simplify the creation of documentation and its later usage. This guarantees that the documentation created in a project is available when the solution is in operation and that the documents can be updated centrally in the event of changes.

Document management in SAP Solution Manager supports release processes and digital signatures on documents. An authorization concept can be implemented to control and monitor access to documents.

The Business Process Repository already contains documentation for the standard processes supplied by SAP, and can be adapted to organization-specific requirements in an SAP Solution Manager project.

E-Learning Management
Learning Maps in SAP Solution Manager can be used to create project-based self-learning courses for users, which employees then can use directly at their workplaces. Existing documentation can be used when new Learning Maps are created. It is also possible to map and provide examples

of business processes with the SAP Tutor simulations. The end-user role concept makes it possible to distribute the Learning Maps as URLs by e-mail to all affected users. This means users only receive the information that is relevant for them, helping to avoid information overload.

Solution Monitoring and Service Desk

SAP Solution Manager provides Solution Monitoring and the Service Desk to ensure well-positioned support in this phase and beyond. Solution Monitoring is used to monitor the IT solution and to identify and clear up bottlenecks, with this process completely automated in some cases. The Service Desk supports you in setting up your support organization, to help users and answer their queries efficiently.

SAP Online Knowledge Products

SAP Online Knowledge Products (OKP) provide-role specific knowledge on updates and enhancements of SAP applications.

Services

SAP GoingLive Check

The *SAP GoingLive Check* reduces risks by proactively identifying potential problems, in particular with regard to performance, availability and maintenance, enabling corrective measures to be taken in good time.

SAP EarlyWatch Check

SAP EarlyWatch Check is a service that helps to analyze the operating system, database, and SAP system proactively with regard to optimum performance and system operation.

CCC Strategy Development

The *CCC Strategy Development* service supports customers in establishing a Customer Competence Center (CCC). One of the results of this service is the definition of the CCC's service portfolio. In addition, possible organizational models are elaborated and evaluated. The breadth of the organization can range from a central structure to local, decentralized structures, separated by region or business area, for example. As part of the services, the necessary roles and the required professional background of the personnel to be used are determined.

SAP Solution Management Assessment

Within the framework of the Premium Engagements, SAP provides the *SAP Solution Management Assessment* service to identify and evaluate availability requirements. In this process, the solution landscape and most important core business processes are analyzed. The result is a technical evaluation of the risks for stability, as well as the availability and safety of the core business processes.

Empowering

Documentation of SAP Product Standards
The documentation of SAP Product Standards can be called up in the SAP Help Portal (*http://help.sap.com*).

4.5 AI5: Procuring IT Resources

In this context, the term "IT resources" means hardware, software, and services. The aim is to integrate the procurement of IT resources in the overall purchasing process of the company. The procurement process is to be implemented in such a way that the IT resources are available at the right time and the right price. The procurement process includes supplier contract management, supplier selection, and the purchasing process itself. The content of contracts regarding maintenance and licensing of intellectual property must also be taken into consideration in the software procurement process. If development resources are purchased externally, it must be ensured that the contracted persons adhere to company guidelines.

Tools

mySAP SRM
mySAP Supplier Relationship Management (mySAP SRM) enables customers to optimize their supplier selection in order to achieve a goal-oriented procurement strategy that adds value and limits procurement time and cost. mySAP SRM also supports external service management and the procurement of development resources.

Services

SAP IT Strategy Development

The *SAP IT Strategy Development: Restructuring and Sourcing* service has the aim of developing sourcing strategies, evaluating financial risks and benefits, and developing a sourcing governance model.

4.6 AI6: Managing Changes

This process formally defines the manner in which changes to the IT solution are processed and monitored. In addition to planned maintenance measures (such as support packages), changes can also be emergency corrective measures that need to be implemented as quickly as possible to rectify a fault in the production environment (using SAP Notes, for example). First, the corresponding procedures and standards for change management must be created. For example, you must ensure that only changes that have been released by a supervisory body can be performed and only changes that have been successfully tested can be imported into the production landscape. The standardized procedures may not be circumvented, necessitating an end-to-end authorization concept.

In addition to the necessary priorities and authorization profiles, you need a procedure for analyzing effects in order to estimate the risks inherent in changes. An accompanying monitoring and reporting procedure is needed until the change has been concluded and documented.

Tools

Change Request Management

Change Request Management in SAP Solution Manager provides a preconfigured standard for managing changes that is oriented towards ITIL Change Management. All changes to a project that are to be implemented within a certain period can be conducted in a planned, monitored manner. Changes that arise outside of project plans and require fast resolution (urgent corrections) can also be documented and implemented efficiently. SAP Solution Manager closes the gap that is present in many other change-management solutions. In addition to the purely administrative workflow, Change Request Management permits seamless integration into the Transport Management System (TMS), allowing the central administration of transport orders. As a result, all steps—from the initial request and authorization procedures to going live—are documented and can be reproduced.

SAP GRC Process Control

Within SAP GRC Process Control, a simulation function analyzes whether data in a transport order contains risks for business processes when imported into the production system. For example, the configuration in a development system may permit postings to be made in a closed period. But if this is against company policy, and checks are implemented in the production environment that explicitly forbid this setting, potential risks can be identified in a simulation of the transport request before faults have occurred. This preventive measure helps to safeguard change processes in accordance with company guidelines.

Services

SAP Solution Manager Roadmap

The *SAP Solution Manager Roadmap* service offers Premium Engagement customers support in the evaluation of SAP Solution Manager scenarios and helps to implement concepts profitably in the company.

Empowering

Change Request Management

SAP offers a multi-day course on the subject of Change Request Management with SAP Solution Manager. This course examines the concepts, architecture, and change processes in detail and trains participants in their use.

SAP Solution Manager Learning Map

As part of the OKP, SAP offers free self-study courses on the complete range of SAP Solution Manager services. The OKPs are available under *http://www.service.sap.com/rkt-solman*.

4.7 AI7: Installing and Accrediting Solutions and Changes

After development is finished, the systems must be put into use. In addition to training specialist personnel, a test and implementation plan must be created. After successfully changing the systems and transferring data, the new changes and solutions must be comprehensively tested, which concludes with a test acceptance process. The creation and implementation of a detailed changeover plan is essential for the success of the new application when it goes live. In addition to authorization concepts, the changeover plan specifies parallel operation for periodic closing operations of important operations.

Appropriate monitoring of the distribution and commissioning of the approved configuration must also be ensured. This requires dual control at the very least and also adherence to the principle of segregation of duties, which means that no single person can be permitted to create, test, and activate a configuration. It must also be possible to document and evaluate changes based on tools. Once the change process has ended, you need to trigger a review to check whether the changes fulfill customer requirements and whether the intended benefits and cost objectives have been achieved.

Tools

Change Request Management

Change Request Management in SAP Solution Manager not only supports the change process itself, but also helps to safeguard the solutions with a comprehensive authorization concept. The scenario uses a configurable dual-control principle, which means the user who has developed a function may not test that function. The project cycle of Change Request Management has a phase structure which offers an operative enhancement of the project plan:

- ▶ Development without release
- ▶ Development with release
- ▶ Test
- ▶ Preparations for going live (Emergency Corrections)
- ▶ Going live

In the *development without release* phase, a transport order can be generated but not released. The release can only happen once the *development with release* phase has been reached. It is started by a central committee (change advisory board or change manager) and allows the release of transports and their import into the test environment. After the project changes have been imported into the test environment, the integration test of the *test* phase can be performed. No more change requests for this project can be created at this stage; only errors which have occurred in the test are corrected. The *preparations for going live* phase (Emergency Corrections) permits users with the appropriate authorization to make further necessary changes before the changes are imported into the production environment in the *going live* phase. Changes that were not successfully tested in the prior test phase cannot be imported.

Test Management in SAP Solution Manager

The Test Workbench of SAP Solution Manager can be used to conduct comprehensive tests. The eCATT enables the performance of automated tests in heterogeneous system landscapes.

Test Data Migration Server

The Test Data Migration Server is used to read out real data from production systems selectively and make this data available as test data in development and test system environments.

System and Data Conversion

SAP provides the Migration Workbench in the standard system to migrate existing data from existing systems. The Migration Workbench is enhanced and supplemented by the tools and services of System Landscape Optimization.

Virsa Compliance Calibrator

Virsa Compliance Calibrator can check that segregation of duties for authorizations has been implemented. "Get clean," for example, prevents a single person from being responsible for configuration, testing, and activation.

Virsa Role Expert

Virsa Role Expert ensures that all roles in a company are consistent and free of conflicts.

Virsa Access Enforcer

Virsa Access Enforcer guarantees that no changes can be made that infringe on the segregation of duties.

5 CobiT Domain: Deliver and Support

The processes that ensure the availability, stability, and performance of the support services for the solution are summarized in the CobiT domain *Deliver and Support* (DS; see Table 5.1). The focus here is on communication between IT management and the business areas, which results in the required quality criteria for services and support. CobiT looks at these processes from the planning of services and criteria to implementing the defined services and measuring their quality.

CobiT			ITSAM Process
Domain	Process	Control	
DS	1	Define and manage Service Levels	Service Level Management, Integration processes
DS	2	Manage third-party services	Service Level Management, Integration processes
DS	3	Manage performance and capacity	Capacity Management, Integration Processes, Operations

CobiT			ITSAM Process
Do-main	Pro-cess	Control	
DS	4	Ensure continuous service	Availability Management, IT Service Continuity Management
DS	5	Ensure systems security	Integration Processes
DS	6	Identify and allocate costs	Financial Management for IT Services
DS	7	Educate and train users	Release Management
DS	8	Manage service desk and incidents	Incident Management
DS	9	Manage the configuration	Configuration Management, Change Management
DS	10	Manage problems	Problem Management
DS	11	Manage data	IT Monitoring, Availability Management,
DS	12	Manage the physical environment	Configuration Management, Change Management, IT Monitoring
DS	13	Manage operations	Operations

Table 5.1 Overview of CobiT Processes in DS and ITSAM

5.1 DS1: Defining and Managing Service Levels

The aim of this process is to define and manage the service levels in such a way that the departments' business requirements of IT are always met. To achieve this, several sub-processes are implemented. The context of the service agreement formally defines how service level management is regulated between provider and customer. You define which services are used to what extent. A service catalog supports the selection of the possible services and their costs. You also describe roles and responsibilities.

In a subsequent process, the type and scope of the available or used services are described. The service level agreement (SLA) defines the mutual agreement regarding which services are used in which quantity, as well as which specific quality criteria have to be met. The costs incurred for these are specified. If applicable, contractual penalties are specified for gross violations of the agreement. An SLA shall include criteria for all used services, in most cases at least availability, downtime management, throughput, data increase, securities, and special request services.

SLAs can be supplemented with operating level agreements (OLA). In the legal sense, an OLA does not constitute a contract. Unlike SLAs, these are internal company agreements. The aim and content of OLAs are comparable to SLAs. Analogously, underpinning contracts can also be made with the service provider to supplement the range of services. However, the SLA partner is the central contact person for the customer. Regular monitoring and reporting of criteria is necessary to determine whether the contractual agreements are fulfilled and to check whether the quality criteria meet the business requirements. The transaction is subject to constant changes. Since SLAs are based on business processes, they are also subject to constant adjustment and optimization. SLAs must be revised at regular intervals based on the latest measurements and analyses carried out.

Tools

Monitoring and Service Level Reporting

The standard deliveries of all SAP applications include preconfigured monitoring tools that already contain possible measurement criteria. Despite all standards, each business process is customer-specific, partly due to the different quantities of data and the different business environments. This results in different requirements of systems operations, as well as different quality criteria and measurement points for the services to be provided in IT management. Therefore, the integrated monitors must be adjusted and enhanced.

CCMS

Transaction RZ20 is available within the Computing Center Management System (CCMS). RZ20 is the CCMS user interface itself; i.e., the monitor display. This transaction is part of the Basis module of every SAP system using SAP NetWeaver Application Server ABAP. In addition to the actual display of the monitors, CCMS also includes transactions for customizing, maintaining, and linking the monitors. Agents—executable programs that collect statistical data from components through interfaces and deliver this data to the monitors (transaction RZ20)—support AS-Java-based solutions, such as Portal, XI, and third-party solutions. You configure the monitoring environment customer-specifically, which means the choice is ultimately up to the customer. SAP recommends using SAP Solution Manager as the central monitoring platform. In general, the data that the SAP agents deliver to CCMS can also be forwarded to external monitoring tools. This also can be done the other way around. Because the business processes are usually not limited to one system, but instead work across systems, you need an integrated view of monitoring. This view is essential to transparent system operations in any case.

Solution Monitoring

In SAP Solution Manager, Solution Monitoring includes the following monitoring functions:

► Central System Administration (CSA) contains action lists for the required, regular administrative tasks in standard solutions. CSA thus performs an initial knowledge transfer and offers a tool for the standardized maintenance of SAP solutions. This knowledge transfer is particularly valuable for new solutions, for which few routines have been established in the system process.

► System Monitoring includes the tools required for establishing a central monitoring system, with automated warning messages for all systems in the environment. Many monitors are already preconfigured, however, you will have to adjust, select, or enhance them for your particular business solution.

▶ SAP Solution Manager supports Business Process Monitoring (BPMon) via a graphical monitoring interface. In contrast to technical monitoring, BPMon monitors the solutions from the business perspective. After all, user departments aren't really interested in whether a server is technically available, for example. What matters is whether the business process is available and working properly. The general overview of the respective business process and the individual business process steps, their reference to the technical systems used, and important technical key performance indicators (KPIs) are displayed on a single screen. BPMon enables the integration of the view of the business processes and the related technical processes.

▶ SAP EarlyWatch Alert (EWA) is a preconfigured, automated service that collects important technical key figures and evaluates them against standardized threshold values. As a result, it generates a report that warns about critical developments and, if applicable, provides hints for avoiding problems.

▶ In the Service Level Reporting (SLR) area, you can use the EWA data and additional current and historical measuring values from the monitoring areas of SAP Solution Manager to compile customer-specific analyses for service level reporting. The statistics can be aggregated and analyzed.

Solution Reporting

Furthermore, Version 4.0 of SAP Solution Manager provides comprehensive functions for Solution Reporting that go far beyond the strictly technical character of Solution Monitoring. They are divided into the following areas:

▶ **Services**

Cover requirements involving the system settings or system/profile parameters and detailed analysis of EWA data

▶ **Administration**

General overview of all systems of a solution and their availability as well as important key figures regarding the quality of system administration

▶ **Service Desk**

Analysis of the status of Service Desk messages (incidents and problems) with reference to the solution in SAP Solution Manager

▶ **Change Management**

Detailed analyses of the status and the number of change entries, corrections and transport requests as well as changes to affected objects

▶ **Issues and Top Issues**

An issue in SAP Solution Manager describes a problem that threatens to affect the business processes in an SAP solution environment. SAP deliberately uses the term "issue" to distinguish it from the ITIL terms "incident" and "problem." According to ITIL, an incident or a problem always involves solutions already in production and affects production business processes. In contrast, an issue is proactive by nature. It involves circumstances that lead to an incident or a problem, and thus to violations of SLAs, and might prevent the production start-up of a solution. This could entail missing expertise regarding the operation of a solution or a missing monitoring tool, because of which an error in the solution would probably be recognized too late, if at all. Issue Management in SAP Solution Manager enables you to document such problems in the context of the solution, organize their processing, and analyze the problem solution process later on.

You can access all data collected by SAP Solution Manager in the different monitoring areas through the integrated SAP NetWeaver Business Intelligence (BI). This enables you to perform detailed analyses and in particular time series analyses over extended periods of time.

Schäfer/Melich 2006[3] provide a detailed description of the functions.

Services

SAP Business Process Management

SAP offers the *Business Process Management* service for implementing proactive monitoring of the most important business processes and steps within SAP Solution Manager. At the same time, the focus is on the optimization of the business processes. For this purpose, suitable business

---

3 Marc Schäfer, Matthias Melich: *SAP Solution Manager*; SAP PRESS, Bonn 2006.

process-oriented key performance indicators (KPIs) are defined and translated into technical checks and measuring points, which is also how the basic data for Service Level Management is determined. The central node, the Management Cockpit, gives you an integrated view of cross-system data processing and the data flows within the business processes.

EarlyWatch

SAP EarlyWatch Alert and *SAP EarlyWatch Check* are standardized SAP services for carrying out product-specific, technical measurements in SAP systems. The determined results are compared to best practice threshold values and analyzed, and recommendations for optimizing systems operations are determined to the extent possible. SAP EarlyWatch Alert is a fully automated service within SAP Solution Manager; EWA usually analyzes the runtime behavior of the system over the past week once a week. The EarlyWatch Check service is a remote service, performed by a support employee in SAP Solution Manager according to the service tools stored there. Because both services are performed within SAP Solution Manager, the results can be processed further in Service Level Reporting. At the same time, both reports are already of a quality that can be used as the first draft of a technical service level report for SAP solutions.

SAP Application Management

The group of *SAP Application Management* services also includes a number of services in which you support the experts in the definition and ongoing maintenance of service-level key figures, as well as measurement and analysis. This includes the provision and setup of the support infrastructure with regard to incident and problem management, change and release management and service level management per se. The services are provided as part of the day-to-day activities, which means your employees can familiarize themselves with everyday tasks and problems with the support of SAP experts. SAP Application Management services therefore support a whole range of CobiT processes and are mentioned repeatedly in the following chapters. They are only described briefly at this point, however.

Empowering

SMO System Administration

In the context of the SAP Premium Engagements, you can use the Solution Management Optimization (SMO) System Administration service to familiarize yourself with the best practices for using analysis monitoring and maintenance tools, especially when switching to and introducing new SAP solutions. The foundation for future monitoring is established.

5.2 DS2: Managing Third-Party Services

It has become common practice to outsource IT services— i.e., buy them from specialized service providers—and no longer perform them in one's own company. In turn, outsourcers use the services of other providers, which can result in quite a complex net of relationships. Figure 5.1 shows the interconnection of different services that can be obtained from different providers.

Irrespective of the source of the services, the most important thing is that the business requirements are met in a stable, high-performance manner.

Hence, a clear role description, clear specification of areas of responsibility, and clearly defined requirements of third-party providers are crucial. CobiT also requires the processes of performance management and third-party provider monitoring to be introduced.

SAP Solution Manager

From SAP's perspective, it is important that the procured services ensure that the solutions operate in a stable, high-performance environment with regard to quality and scope. Here, SAP Solution Manager is the central tool for IT service and application management. In the context of managing the services of all involved parties including third-party providers, you also need to clarify how SAP Solution Manager is going to be used. For example, you could use a central, joint SAP Solution Manager system. But each provider can also use its own, local SAP Solution Manager. You can configure the exchange of data between different instances of SAP Solution Manager.

Figure 5.1 ▶
Network of Service Provider and Customer Relationships

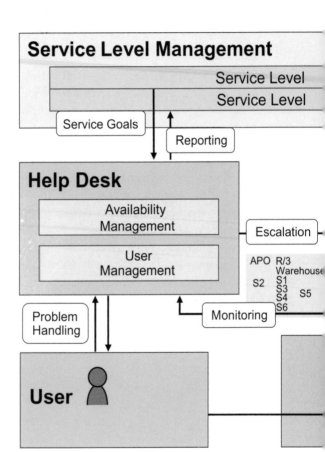

Customer
Business Process Owner

Service Level Management

Service Level

Service Level

Service Goals

Reporting

Help Desk

Availability
Management

User
Management

Escalation

APO   R/3
            Warehouse
S2   S1
       S3
       S4   S5
       S6

Problem
Handling

Monitoring

User

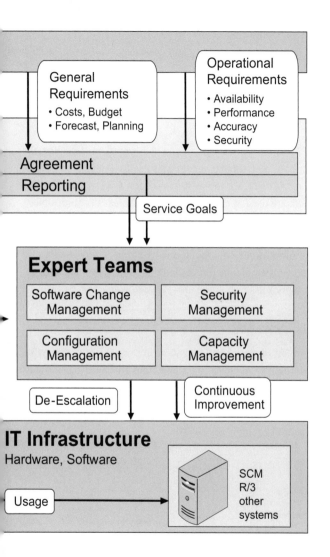

Monitoring Tools

The tools for monitoring and service level reporting also offer functions for managing third-party providers. However, you have to define who can use the tools and how.

Services

SAP Consulting supports your customers in designing the supply and service relationships with third-party providers. In doing so, the processes of the ITSAM framework or ITIL are used as the basis for defining areas of responsibility, developing a service portfolio, assigning tasks and competencies, and specifying control parameters. The functional and non-functional requirements of the IT services are also documented, which provides a basis for contractual agreements and SLAs, as well for IT controlling.

Empowering

Anderhub 2006[4] provides some important notes as to what should be included in an SLA from the SAP solution perspective. He describes several tools and how they are used in the process of service level reporting.

---

4   Anderhub, Vital: *Service Level Management—the ITIL Process in SAP Operations*; SAP PRESS Essentials 21, SAP PRESS, Bonn 2006.

5.3 DS3: Managing Performance and Capacity

Performance and capacity management generate forecasts for the future development of performance and capacity in relation to business development. As a first step, you should implement suitable measurements. Having this information available permanently helps you to optimize costs and stabilize an existing solution. You can use the generated forecasts to detect hardware and software bottlenecks early on and resolve them before they cause problems. In contrast to ITIL, CobiT places more emphasis on permanent performance monitoring. In SAP IT Service & Application Management (ITSAM), special attention is paid to the integration processes and their increasing role in the implementation of SAP NetWeaver solutions. Performance Management is one of the processes that is located on the interface between application and IT management.

Tools

The active performance and capacity management required in DS usually exceeds standard service level monitoring and reporting.

SAP Solution Manager and Monitoring

There is no such strict distinction in the monitoring tools supplied by SAP and SAP Solution Manager, however. SAP regards service level monitoring and management as a part of the overall available monitoring. Hence, the same tools are used as described under *DS1—Service Level Definition and Management*. The challenge is to define and use suitable monitor collections. The corresponding measurements and analyses are preconfigured.

Central Performance History

You can use the Central Performance History (CPH) to record trends in selected measured values across specific intervals, and also to generate forecasts.

Service Level Reporting

The Service Level Reporting function also allows you to generate reports that are limited to capacity and performance management.

Services

EarlyWatch

Here, you can also use services that support service level management. The *EarlyWatch Alert* and *EarlyWatch Check* already provide some statistical forecasts for the future development of measured values. If necessary, you can add additional measured values and forecasts.

Empowering

SMO System Administration

The *Solution Management Optimization (SMO) System Administration* service in the context of the SAP Premium Engagements, mentioned above in *DS1—Defining and Managing Service Levels,* can be useful here, as well. It deals with useful KPIs and their measurement and analysis, in addition to the handling of the tools.

5.4 DS4: Ensuring Continuous Operation

To ensure operational reliability, continuous service performance—and therefore stable system operation—must be guaranteed permanently. But the CobiT requirements and corresponding control objectives exceed this. To ensure stable operation, you have to prepare for future events, risk situations, or even disasters. This includes planning how business processes can be continued, even if potentially restricted, in a worst-case scenario, and analyzing which resources are actually critical for business. At a minimum, a framework for IT continuity for the worst case also has to be elaborated, tested, and spread, and training must be provided for the methods considered necessary. Aside from these emergency plans and activities, the secure storage of backups at a separate, safe location is also part of the CobiT control objectives.

Tools

CCMS Weekly Plan
Within CCMS, particularly important database-administration activities such as backup and the maintenance of database statistics can be scheduled weekly. The results and logs for the activities are also available within CCMS.

EarlyWatch Alert

The EarlyWatch Alert report analyzes and evaluates the regularity and correctness of the activities by means of the provided logs. In doing so, the standard backup frequencies and storage periods suggested by SAP are used as the basis for comparison.

Services

IT Continuity Management

The *IT Continuity Management* service helps you discover the causes of a system failure. Technical and organizational weak points are analyzed and action lists for improvements are compiled.

Empowering

SAP IT Excellence Enablement

In the context of SAP IT Excellence Enablement, SAP offers two training and certification programs aimed at site profiles:

► **SAP NetWeaver Management**

The *SAP NetWeaver Management* course introduces the new architecture and the structure of the system environment as well as best practices for system management, such as important KPIs, monitoring, problem analysis and solution, configuration, setup of a development environment, background processing, security aspects, and user and authorization profiles. This knowledge is the prerequisite for providing corresponding services as an operating outsourcer.

► **SAP Application Management**
The *SAP Application Management* course covers SAP application change management, business process monitoring, and the monitoring and evaluation of the performance of business processes.

Best Practices
Within SAP Solution Manager, best-practice documents are available for backup and recovery from the technical and the application perspective. The recommended procedures for different SAP applications are described.

5.5 DS5: Ensuring Systems Security

Ensuring systems security is a particularly important CobiT control. Within ITIL, IT Security Management is given a separate area and therefore its own publication volume. A separate ISO standard has been set up for certifying systems security (for example, ISO 270001).

The basis for stable systems security is an IT security plan that covers the different areas of security, specifies the security policy, and prescribes monitoring measures. User administration is not the only important area. Other important areas are network management, security in the exchange of classified data, encryption techniques, and the monitoring of the actual security software and technologies. Moreover, the processes of the security tests and comprehensive monitoring also belong to the DS5 control. At the start of implementation, you have to specify how an incident is defined in the system security environment.

Tools

In line with the significance of system security in application operations, SAP offers powerful tools for managing users and their authorizations.

Authorizations and Roles

The authorization concept within NetWeaver Application Server ABAP forms the foundation. By default, SAP ships preconfigured collections of authorizations, called profiles, for the typical areas of responsibility for business. You can create your specific roles based on this, and you can even define your own authorizations; e.g., for transactions that you have developed yourself. This includes functions for the mass maintenance and the central maintenance of user data. An information system for the evaluation of authorizations and user access is also part of the functional scope.

SAP User Management Engine

For SAP NetWeaver, the User Management Engine (UME) has been introduced for SAP NetWeaver AS Java and SAP NetWeaver Portal. UME implements central user and authorization management for the SAP Java solutions. If you wish, you can also use the Lightweight Directory Access Protocol (LDAP), the database assigned to AS Java or ABAP user management to manage user data. The UME functions are comparable to those of the SAP NetWeaver ABAP environment. In a solution environment in which SAP NetWeaver Java and SAP NetWeaver ABAP are used, Java, and ABAP user management work together synchronously.

Single Sign-on

The concept behind the Single Sign-on (SSO) is that users only have to log on once to gain access to all systems. SAP NetWeaver supports the required technologies.

Security Audit Log

SAP provides the Security Audit Log specifically for auditors. You configure profiles to define which information and activities are to be recorded. Users with system-critical authorizations are usually of particular interest. The Security Audit Log may contain user-specific data, which might require coordination between the data protection officer and the personnel officer.

Audit Information System

The SAP Audit Information System (AIS) supports the analysis of several different security packages, as well as monitoring.

SAP GRC Access Control

SAP GRC Access Control helps companies avoid security risks that can be caused by the assignment of access authorizations. The most important thing to consider is how much responsibility may be given to one person, and therefore to one user profile. SAP GRC Access Control enables you to automate the analysis of all access authorizations for possible violations of the segregation of duties in the company.

▶ **Virsa Compliance Calibrator**

Virsa Compliance Calibrator represents the core of SAP GRC Access Control. It analyzes the access authorizations across enterprise application software systems such as SAP and other non-SAP ERP systems. It has the most comprehensive, flexible rules library available and compares the actual state of the systems to this best-practice library. You can use this function to analyze access risks across the company.

▶ **Virsa Role Expert**

Virsa Role Expert helps the IT organization and the departments in designing new roles. It helps you ensure that business functions are consistently segregated and all roles are clearly documented from the start of the design phase. This prevents risks from entering the productive environment.

▶ **Virsa FireFighter for SAP**

Users who temporarily receive the "SAP_ALL" authorization in production environments are a high security risk. This authorization allows users to manipulate or even delete all programs and data, for example. Virsa FireFighter for SAP can be used to issue restricted privileged user authorizations (FireFighter IDs). If a user uses a Virsa FireFighter ID, all activities are logged in a format that is easy for auditors to read. In addition, a workflow is triggered in which all activities are subsequently analyzed.

- ▶ **Virsa Access Enforcer**

  Maintaining authorizations is a constant source of security risk. Authorizations have to be maintained when employees are hired, leave the company, or switch to different roles within the company. During these maintenance activities, Virsa Access Enforcer checks that the authorizations granted are not too comprehensive and do not pose a business risk with respect to segregation of duties. Virsa Access Enforcer guides the approval process for access requests, prevents risks by informing managers about potential access risks, and guides them through the remediation process to ensure ongoing compliance.

SAP GRC Process Control

SAP GRC Process Control monitors the business transactions in the application layer down to the technology stack. For example, analyses of financial limits for individual employees' business transactions can be deployed in business processes. SAP GRC Process Control monitors configuration controls, as well as master data controls. IT infrastructure monitoring is also integrated through a development partnership with Cisco. For example, the data movements at the network level are analyzed using security-management tools, and then made available in SAP GRC Process Control remediation and reporting functionality. Management can use a dashboard to quickly get an overview of all security-relevant aspects of the company, and evaluate the status of the correction measures that have been introduced.

Figure 5.2 shows a possible analysis.

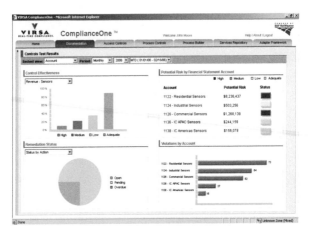

Figure 5.2 Evaluation of the Control Status During the Checked Period

Services

An active Security and Risk Management focus group operates at SAP. Experts from consulting, product management, development, and enterprise security meet regularly from around the world to exchange experiences. This group has developed SAP's service offerings and will elaborate them further based on customer feedback. Customers receive support in recognizing and implementing the required security aspects for operating SAP applications. The service offerings are explained in the following sections.

Security Strategy Consulting

The first step in *Security Strategy Consulting* involves compiling an inventory, which includes the areas of risk management processes, site and legal requirements, SAP authorization concept, and implementation of SAP-specific security features. Based on this, gaps in the security strategy are listed and analyzed, and recommendations on resolving them are provided.

Security for Enterprise SOA

The *Security for Enterprise SOA* service supports the implementation of security solutions for web services in the context of the Enterprise Service-Oriented Architecture (Enterprise SOA).

Governance Risk Management and Compliance Solution

Quick Start is a consulting offer for implementing SAP Compliance Calibrator, Role Expert, and Access Enforcer. During this service, the GRC Access Control components are installed, and application examples are implemented. These examples are used to illustrate how the implementation of GRC Access Control supports SOX-relevant processes.

Technical Risk Assessment

In the *Technical Risk Assessment for an SAP Environment* service, the SAP environment (including the used internet scenarios) is checked for security risks, based on the handbook for the SAP NetWeaver Portal, using automatic tools such as Watchfire AppScan, ISS Scanner, and so on.

Identification and Access Management

The service for identification and access management helps you create a comprehensive identification and access solution across the entire organization. Here, the focus is on migrating the authorization concepts in the individual SAP applications to a single, integrated solution that is tailored to the customer's needs.

SAP Authorization Concepts

The *SAP Authorization Concepts* service helps you design and swiftly implement a transparent, easy-to-maintain SAP role concept. As an enhancement, it is possible to check the degree to which existing authorization concepts meet the SOX requirements.

Security Optimization Service

SAP offers the *Security Optimization* service in the context of the Premium Engagements. In the variant of the fully automated self service in SAP Solution Manager, users and—in particular—system-critical standard users such as SAP* and DDIC are checked, along with their passwords. The distribution of critical authorizations in the system is also checked. The results are compared to the recommendations from the SAP Security Guidelines and analyzed with regard to the resulting risk. Interfaces, their users, and access data are checked accordingly. Alternatively, this service can also be performed by an SAP employee, who can pay more attention to customer-specific solutions.

Empowering

SAP Security Guidelines

The SAP Security Guidelines are checklists for the most important security aspects affecting the various SAP solutions. Further notes will be made available for the implementation of the security environments.

5.6 DS6: Identifying and Allocating Costs

The precise recording of IT costs and an agreement with the business areas regarding the fair allocation of these costs are prerequisites for a functioning IT controlling structure. The requested and required IT services are defined, and costs are calculated. Efficient cost, resources, and investment controlling are established based on these figures. These values are included in the pricing for IT services. The costs are allocated based on the exact activity allocation.

Tools

cProjects

Using the SAP standard functionality, you can define and allocate IT services as "products" and allocate the actual acceptance through the business area. One-time IT projects are mapped using cProjects, SAP's tool for operational project management. The costs of the IT project are assigned to the project account, using the integration with the SAP personnel system and accounting. The status of the project—actual costs, commitments, and remaining budget—is analyzed using standard reports.

5.7 DS7: Educating and Training Users

An analysis of the training requirement is a key prerequisite for the effective education and training of users. Furthermore, in addition to the requirements of the applications' users, you need to register the education requirement, and develop corresponding education concepts in service support and service delivery. The education needs can be met using different training methods, such as self-study with e-learning or in-class training. The most important thing is to measure the training success, by evaluating relevance, quality, effectiveness, and costs.

Tools

SAP Tutor

SAP Tutor significantly contributes to delivering knowledge in a very customer-specific, goal-oriented manner. Each use of a transaction is recorded, while handling and backgrounds are explained at the same time. Once use is recorded, the users can call up the recordings individually. SAP offers complete recordings for standard applications. SAP Tutor and the instructions recorded therein are an ideal supplement to general courses and documentation.

E-Learning Management in SAP Solution Manager

With E-Learning Management, SAP Solution Manager enables you to generate user courses for new or changed processes in projects or solutions and make these available to the users as e-learning materials. Learning Maps can be distributed across the organizations in URL form and contain different learning units, such as SAP Tutor lessons, documents etc.

SAP Knowledge Management

SAP offers a special software solution for knowledge management, SAP Knowledge Management (KM). It is a crucial part of information management in SAP NetWeaver. In the training area, it is especially effective in managing the knowledge objects.

SAP Learning Solution

The SAP Learning Solution covers all relevant education processes in the business and is fully integrated with mySAP ERP. In this approach, the solution connects learning and business processes and enables holistic education management that can be modeled on the enterprise strategy. Education processes can be displayed together and integrated into personnel administration, personnel development, organization, and cost accounting.

Services

SAP Help Portal

General descriptions of the functions and use of all SAP products are available in the *SAP Help Portal* (*http://help. sap.com*). The documentation is shipped to customers in electronic form together with the software and is available as an online library in the SAP systems.

Empowering

Training and E-Learning

SAP offers extensive training programs at numerous locations around the world. The courses are given via classes with one or more instructors. In addition to the courses offered by SAP, several courses are available as e-learning materials in electronic form. Please see the SAP Service Marketplace for more information.

5.8　DS8: Managing the Service Desk and Incidents

According to ITIL, the Service Desk serves as the single point of contact for users. All incidents that affect production business operations, as well as other queries, are reported to the Service Desk and managed and processed as incidents for the time being. A well-planned and well-managed Service Desk with a stable incident management process is a prerequisite for helping users promptly and effectively. Incoming incidents are classified and prioritized according to different criteria.

The main objective of incident management is to avoid or resolve disruptions to a business process flow as efficiently as possible. A solution database is used to achieve this. From the incident-management perspective, the incident is also considered resolved if the user can be shown a workaround. Incidents are forwarded to Problem Management for further analysis of the causes and, ultimately, problem resolution.

Tools

With Service Desk, the SAP Solution Manager provides an end-to-end tool for carrying out the processes of incident and problem management. At the same time, SAP Solution Manager offers an expert tool for analyzing problems and solving them for the entire system environment: SAP Solution Manager Diagnostics.

SAP Solution Manager Service Desk

The *Service Desk* of SAP Solution Manager is a trouble-ticket system that can be adjusted to individual customer needs from a preconfigured standard. It is integrated into all relevant functions of SAP Solution Manager and the connected satellite systems. Incidents during operation can be forwarded to the Service Desk directly from the respective application. The Service Desk automatically forwards these support messages to the correct point in the support organization. Technical background information, which facilitates message processing, is made available automatically for the most part. Tools such as the Notes Search in the SAP Service Marketplace are also integrated into the Service Desk functions.

Messages from the customer-support organization, such as a customer competence center, can be forwarded to SAP Active Global Support directly without any loss of information. Service Desk makes the relevant information available centrally to all parties involved in the process at all times, and offers the option of creating a customized solution database. It is also possible to connect a trouble ticket system from a third-party provider.

IT Help Desk with SAP CRM Interaction Center

With mySAP CRM Interaction Center, you can accept general IT-related, incident, and problem messages, as well as user queries, from several interaction channels in one IT Help Desk. The integration of e-mail response management and the integration of customer web-based forms allow the automated processing and documentation of simple queries as well as the goal-oriented pre-qualification and assignment of complex questions. In general, a special user interface allows problem messages to be classified into several levels, assigned to technical components, and processed in a standardized way. Reaction and escalation times can be determined from service contracts, and can be made available for processing the respective incident in the form of service level agreements. Processing times can be recorded case-specifically and be used for further processing, up to the invoicing of the solution.

Multi-level problem solution processes can be mapped by means of (partially) automated, rule-based forwarding, in which the rules are maintained with the same rule editor as e-mail routing. Alternatively, SAP Business Workflow can be used for message forwarding. Integrated CRM service processes can be used to bundle several incidents in a higher level problem case and process them together. Aside from interaction-centric and process-centric analyses, reporting also offers integrated key figures, such as the average call

duration and the average amount of interaction for each
problem category.

Empowering

SAP Solution Manager 4.0: Service Desk
The SAP Solution Manager 4.0: Service Desk course lasts
two days, and gives you an overview of the functions of
Service Desk and its configuration options. You learn the
basics and specifics of message processing, connecting external help desk systems, and best practices.

Incident Management
Incident Management is a four-hour e-learning unit that ex-
plains the basic functions of Service Desk in SAP Solution
Manager.

5.9 DS9: Managing the Configuration

Ultimately, configuration management must be based on
the requirements of the business processes. In doing so, you
need to clarify which configuration items and relationships
exist. There are often relationships between objects that
you have to take into account when changing a configuration item. Accordingly, ITIL requires a special Configuration
Management Database in which all relevant configuration
items (CIs) and their relationships are recorded. The aim of
this process is to prevent downtimes due to unpredicted
side effects; e.g., by controlling the configuration items and
the changes made to them.

Tools

From the SAP perspective, different classes of CIs can be formed, such as ABAP instance parameters, Java Engine parameters, Customizing, authorizations, settings in interfaces, and even programming objects such as releases and support packages. According to the particularities of the different CIs, specific tools are available for maintenance and analysis.

Change Request Management

Changes to configuration items are handled the same way as normal changes and are thus best implemented according to change management. SAP offers Change Request Management within SAP Solution Manager to map this process.

System Landscape Directory

The System Landscape Directory (SLD) is the central approach used by SAP for managing CIs and their relationships, in particular with used releases, support packages, versions of interfaces, and programming objects in SAP NetWeaver. To do so, SLD basically uses the standard for the data model and the description language of the common information model (CIM), as defined by the Distributed Management Task Force (DMTF). Through use of these specifications, corresponding information from other systems using this description language can be integrated and data can be exchanged. SLD enables you to administer and analyzes centrally.

Services

EarlyWatch Alert

The report from the *EarlyWatch Alert* provides an overview of important information about used releases and support packages of the different applications. In addition, the parameter settings in relation to the throughput are checked and changes are suggested, if appropriate.

5.10 DS10: Managing Problems

Analyzing problems to identify the actual cause is a crucial part of the problem-management process. With the transition to service-oriented architectures such as SAP NetWeaver, an entirely new type of analysis tool is needed. In conventional client-server architecture, users could easily see the system where the problem occurred. Today's combination of different services in a portal means these system-assignments are lost. The person responsible for support must first determine in which system the problem occurs. The complex operation of problem analysis in SOA is called root-cause analysis. Appropriate tools and qualified employees must be available to solve problems. Effective problem management is an important part of an SLA for ensuring the availability and performance of the business processes, and contributes greatly to customer satisfaction.

Tools

We distinguish between two categories of tools offered for problem management: suitable tools for implementing the process, and tools to solve the problem itself.

SAP Solution Manager Service Desk

SAP recommends using the Service Desk as the basis for the problem management process, as it lets you map and seamlessly link the incident and problem-management processes. The integration into Change Request Management is also possible and recommended.

Issue Management

As a proactive component, SAP Solution Manager also offers Issue Management, which was already mentioned in Section 5.1.1. Issues cover the process seamlessly, from recording to resolution. Within an issue, you can enter tasks, assign them to employees, assign Service Desk messages, and request SAP experts for a problem area (Expert-on-Demand). Issues are therefore one of the central objects for the collaboration between customers and SAP. All measures taken to avoid a problem are documented centrally and can be evaluated using the built-in reporting functions.

SAP NetWeaver Administrator

The SAP NetWeaver Administrator tool is part of the standard delivery of every SAP NetWeaver solution. It is designed for the regular maintenance, monitoring, and troubleshooting of the applications. SAP NetWeaver Administrator bundles the different analysis tools from the ABAP and Java environments at a central point. Support employees no longer have to switch between systems and tools to trace a problem in the system environment.

SAP Solution Manager Diagnostics

Solution Manager Diagnostics has been developed within SAP Solution Manager specifically for the requirements of modern AS Java applications. In addition to the analysis tools for the different components in a SAP NetWeaver system environment, Solution Manager Diagnostics is enhanced with the tools Wily Introscope and Mercury Loadrunner in a form configured specifically for SAP applications. SAP thus gives support experts a powerful tool, but one that requires profound knowledge of the SAP NetWeaver architecture and the way it works.

Solution Manager Diagnostics enables efficient and safe root-cause analysis of problems in customer solutions and is available on a central platform with SAP Solution Manager. Standardized procedures for diagnostics, which are an integral part of SAP NetWeaver, enable safe support because no changes are made. Since Solution Manager Diagnostics allows analyses via an HTTP connection in the browser, no access to the operating system is necessary. Solution Manager Diagnostics does not use the SAP NetWeaver administration tools. Customers control changes to the production environment, which are made using SAP NetWeaver Administrator. In other words, Solution Manager Diagnostics is used for analysis and planning of measures, and SAP NetWeaver Administrator is used to implement the required measures.

The processing status is reported to Solution Manager Diagnostics.

Services

SMO System Administration

In the context of the Premium Engagements, SAP offers the *SMO System Administration* service, which also covers the handling and goal-oriented use of the available tools (such as SAP NetWeaver Administrator and Solution Manager Diagnostics).

5.11 DS11: Managing Data

Data flows are the core of every business process. CobiT Control DS11 focuses on its protection and consistency. Every business process has quality and quantity requirements on data management. If the volume of data to be processed increases, for example, the resources provided for storage, backup, and network throughput have to be adjusted accordingly.

Tools

Relational database management systems (RDBMS) are used most commonly for data management in SAP solutions. Within software lifecycle management, SAP offers tools for analyzing and evaluation the database with regard to the size of data in the objects.

SAP Quick Sizer

Estimating the volume of data and therefore the required throughput is especially necessary in the implementation of new data. In SAP Quick Sizer, which is available on the SAP Service Marketplace, you can estimate the expected volume of data by entering the expected scales of your business objects.

Archiving

The database is designed for collecting and administering data, but if the volume of data becomes too large, this complicates system management, incurring additional risks and costs. To counteract this, SAP systems include archiving algorithms. The data is not deleted from access, but instead moved to the archive, where it remains readable.

Services

EarlyWatch Alert

The EarlyWatch Alert report regularly analyzes database size and growth. Warning messages are sent whenever critical values and corresponding forecasts are encountered.

CCMS

Existing monitors within CCMS are used to monitor space requirements and available space. You can enhance these monitors with threshold values and connect automatic reaction methods, if appropriate.

SMO Data Management Optimization

The dataset to be managed is to be viewed in the following two aspects:

1. Which of the data to be managed is actually required? Once data reaches a certain age, it is usually no longer changed. Alternatively, you might not want any changes, in which case you would need to find suitable archiving objects and archive the involved data.

2. What causes data growth? Is the generated and saved data really useful? Sometimes, especially for controlling, statistics are generated that are never analyzed. An analysis is the first step to avoiding needless saving of data.

These subjects are covered by SMO Data Management Optimization in the context of the Premium Engagements.

SMO Data Archiving Optimization

If an archiving strategy already exists, but does not produce the desired results, you need a detailed analysis in order to use the full potential. The SMO Data Archiving Optimization service, part of the Premium Engagements, performs this task. An archiving strategy might be ineffective because connected business objects are not archived completely. You need to plan and implement a reorganization strategy for certain RDBMSes to ensure that the space that has been freed up by the archiving process can actually be assigned again without restrictions.

Empowering

Training for System Administrators

SAP offers a curriculum for system administrators that teaches the structure and basic operator functions of the CCMS monitor, agent technology, and steps for setting up central monitoring.

5.12 DS12: Managing the Physical Environment

Ultimately, IT management also involves management of the technical equipment. This includes not only computers but all peripheral devices, network technology, and technical access facilities, as well as the physical location of the technology and the power supply. To ensure that business processes run error-free, the technical devices must also be protected from damage and unauthorized access. This entails the definition and implementation of different security areas and the location of critical equipment, such as the physical protection from environmental influences and unauthorized access to highly sensitive measuring devices. The requirements of the technical equipment and its future management must be taken into account when planning and implementing software solutions. This includes processes dealing with applying for, approving, logging, and monitoring personnel access. If necessary, enterprise guidelines, specifications by providers of technical devices, and security requirements and health guidelines must be taken into account. Technical devices must also be protected against harmful environmental influences.

Tools

CCMS also includes some monitoring tools for hardware-oriented components. The monitoring of all sorts of technical equipment is not a central SAP topic, however; so SAP only provides corresponding tools to a limited extent.

5.13 DS13: Managing Operations

From the CobiT perspective, this control includes the definition, implementation, execution, and maintenance of all operation processes. Job scheduling, as a separate process, plays a special role. The required jobs for background processing must be scheduled as evenly as possible, taking business requirements into account at the same time. You need to define the required reaction in case of a termination: who needs which authorizations to schedule or change jobs, for example. Finally, you also need a suitable tool to implement these procedures.

Output devices are another key focus. It is not uncommon to find issues with particular authorization requirements or time-sensitive printing within the business processes. To model these, you might have to meet some technical prerequisites based on required availability or security precautions. You need to develop and establish a concept for the maintenance of the used hardware elements.

Tools

Software Lifecycle Management

Software lifecycle management integrates all tools that are required for the entire lifecycle of a solution, from the implementation to everyday operations. This also includes managing and making required changes and upgrades. Software lifecycle management includes the following key areas:

▶ Installation, upgrade, and license management

▶ Tools and services for solution monitoring and problem analysis

▶ Tools for testing

▶ Customizing and configuration

▶ Data archiving

You can use SAP Solution Manager as the central cockpit for these tools.

Job Scheduler

With SAP NetWeaver, SAP also delivers a job scheduler based on Redwood Cronacle: SAP Central Job Scheduling by Redwood. Integrating Cronacle with SAP NetWeaver gives you access to information about background jobs in the SAP systems as well as in Cronacle. This is particularly useful when SAP Solution Manager is used as the central operations cockpit, because cross-system information about background activities is also available in SAP Solution Manager.

Output Management System

CCMS allows the seamless connection of external output management systems (OMS) to SAP applications. We recommend using OMS in particular for availability-sensitive printouts. These systems are designed exclusively for managing output in a goal-oriented, high performance manner. Accordingly, they usually have an advantage over the SAP Spool System. In addition, they relieve the strain on SAP applications by shifting output management and control.

Services

SAP Solution Manager Starter Pack

This service combines initial Customizing with an introduction to SAP Solution Manager. As the result, crucial function areas of SAP Solution Manager are activated, and basic settings have already been made for the management of their specific system environment and solution.

System Operation

In the *SMO System Administration* service, part of the Premium Engagements, your employees are not only trained in everyday operation, but also learn to maintain a system maintenance action plan (SMAP).

Monitoring

Different monitoring tools help you set up a specific monitoring infrastructure and select suitable KPIs.

Empowering

Best practices also help you with questions regarding job scheduling for complex, time-critical activities.

Best practices have also been developed for monitoring; they are published in Schulz 2004[5].

5 Schulz, Corina: *Conception and Installation of System Monitoring Using the SAP Solution Manager*; SAP PRESS Essentials 2, SAP PRESS, Bonn 2005.

6 CobiT Domain: Monitor and Evaluate

CobiT and ITIL work on process classification with regard to the levels non-existent, initial, repeatable, defined, controlled and measurable, and optimized. This applies to all IT governance processes. To classify the IT processes and identify optimization potential, the processes must be monitored and measured continually. Suitable quality criteria, such as performance and compliance, must be defined with statutory and other specifications. Only then can quality improvement be included in the life cycle of IP processes as a continuous process.

CobiT			ITSAM Process
Do-main	Pro-cess	Control	
ME	1	Monitor and evaluate IT performance	All ITSAM processes
ME	2	Monitor and evaluate internal controls	All ITSAM processes

CobiT			ITSAM Process
Do-main	Pro-cess	Control	
ME	3	Ensure regulatory compliance	Configuration Management, Release Management, Change Management, IT Service Continuity Management
ME	4	Provide IT governance	All ITSAM processes

Table 6.1 Overview of CobiT Processes in ME and ITSAM

6.1 ME1: Monitoring and Evaluating IT Performance

Permanent monitoring ensures that IT services are effectively monitored. The relevant service indicators must be integrated into systematic, real-time reporting.

When evaluating the IT services, you should consider the following questions:

▸ To what extent is the processing of the business processes supported by the provision of the IT service?

▸ What contribution does the IT service make towards achieving the strategic business plan and the IT plan?

▸ Does the delivery of the IT service comply with statutory and company regulations?

- How does the delivery of the IT services affect internal and external customer satisfaction?

- What are the main IT services for which management reporting is to be performed?

- What future investments can be derived?

- Do new technologies have to be implemented?

- Are investments to be made in new infrastructures or staff training?

In addition, if measured figures deviate from targets, are corrective measures to be introduced? Monitoring is necessary to ensure that the correct measures have been taken and that they comply with the specified statutory and company regulations.

Tools

The implementation of standard SAP applications in mySAP ERP, mySAP CRM, SAP NetWeaver Business Intelligence, and Strategic Enterprise Management enables you to map IT management and the delivery of IT services. The IT services have been defined as products. The transfer prices for the IT services have been calculated and stored. Open interfaces enable you to determine the actual quantities ordered. By evaluating this information, you can use management reporting to map the adherence to service contracts and service plans.

IT Management Reporting

Along with IT Management Reporting for business, you also should establish technically oriented IT Management Reporting. One particularly relevant figure is adherence to Service Level Agreements (SLAs). Based on the SAP Early-Watch Alert evaluations and additional data from the available technical monitoring in SAP Solution Manager, you can call up reporting for the applications and the affected business processes.

SAP GRC Access Control

In order to limit risk, SAP GRC Access Control products ensure that IT staff members are provided with appropriate authorization profiles, enabling them to operate the IT infrastructure needed to run the business processes. At the same time, SAP GRC Access Control eliminates the risks involved in granting authorizations that violate segregation of duties.

SAP GRC Process Control

SAP GRC Process Control is used to document and deploy internal controls. A pool of controls to be checked is distributed to the persons responsible, and any discrepancies are removed by means of remediation cases. One example would be safeguarding purchasing processes for IT resources. Among other things, SAP GRC Process Control can be used to determine whether the supplier's bank data has been changed, or whether an invoice has been settled more than once. It is also possible to check, for example, whether three quotations were obtained from different suppliers before a supplier was selected.

In case of a deficiency or non-adherence to a control, remediation cases are automatically created, assigned priorities, and assigned to the relevant process owners. With this risk-based approach, the deficiencies in the control system are assigned priorities, and cases are monitored until the deficiencies are removed.

6.2 ME2: Monitoring and Evaluating Internal Controls

An important area of monitoring is the use of suitable tools and measures in order to provide targeted management reporting of deviations from the internal controls. The deviations can be disclosed by standard reports, self-evaluation, or reviews by third parties. Monitoring is used mainly to safeguard IT operation effectively and efficiently.

The core features of monitoring are:

▶ Compliance with laws and regulations

▶ The performance of IT processes

▶ Information security

▶ Adherence to checkpoints for Change Management

▶ Adherence to SLAs

The result is that the corresponding correction measures are introduced for all the deviations reported, and their success is monitored.

Tools

SAP GRC Process Control

SAP GRC Process Control is integrated into the control documentation of the SAP GRC Repository. The GRC Repository contains all regulations, risks and controls, test plans, and results, regardless of source system. The SAP GRC Repository provides tools for monitoring and managing controls and risks throughout the enterprise.

SAP GRC Process Control provides managers with a *Global Control Risk Heat Map* to uniquely identify risks and infractions of the internal control system, making it easier for management and auditors to prioritize and introduce corrective measures, and to prevent weak points from developing in the control environment. Figure 6.1 shows an example of the Global Control Risk Heat Map. The regions in a geographical overview are highlighted in various colors to indicate their risk levels. You can choose a region and branch to the next level of detail. On the most detailed level, you get a statistical overview of the financial transactions in a single location: Atlanta in the example. In this case, the total exceeds the defined limit and is therefore highlighted in red.

The checking and remediation activities are transferred to the persons responsible by means of a workflow. The check can be performed manually or automatically. A manual check could specify, for example, that an auditor has to check 15 listed documents, following the dual-control principle. The checking operation is then documented in SAP GRC Process Control.

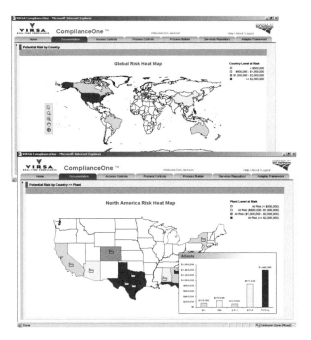

Figure 6.1 Global Control Risk Heat Map

Automatic tests can also be performed. The evaluation of the application-specific controls can determine, for example, whether critical supplier data such as upper limits for orders or payment methods have been changed. SAP GRC Process Control enables automated control monitoring for SAP and non-SAP business applications.

SAP's collaboration with Cisco allows you to set up automatic controls on the network level. You can thus intercept e-mails containing sensitive information before they leave the confines of the company, for example. This protects private information about customers (such as Social Security of other social insurance information), and can also be used to ensure that business figures are not sent out of the company by e-mail before the quarterly figures are published. Cisco also extends the reach of SAP GRC Process Control to include data exchange among all participants in your companies' value chain, including suppliers and customers.

Service Level Reporting

Service Level Reporting in SAP Solution Manager is based on the EWA data and can be enhanced by adding data from monitoring. It forms the interface between IT departments and the business-process owner. By incorporating Business Process Monitoring, you can include business process alerts in Service Level Reporting. In this case, Service Level Reporting provides not only technical information, but also information as to whether technical problems have affected business processes. System-availability reporting is also possible, as well as reporting on system performance, query performance, and database performance, to name just a few possibilities.

Change Request Management

Change Request Management enables you to centrally control—from within SAP Solution Manager—that only approved change requests are implemented, and that they are transported through the system landscape in line with the company-specific schedules and guidelines.

Services

Identity and Access Management Strategy Evaluation

Identity and Access Management Strategy primarily involves analyzing requirements with regard to user registration and access management. The requirements are compared with the quotation from SAP and partner solutions. Alternative solutions are presented and evaluated. Finally, an implementation plan is presented.

Technical Risk Assessment

The result of this service shows the most important technical risks of an implemented SAP landscape and the connected internet-based scenarios. Recommendations for risk removal and minimization are made.

6.3 ME3: Ensuring Compliance with Specifications

An independent review process ensures compliance with laws and regulations. An audit charter is created and the process of engaging an independent auditor is assured. The first step is to identify the applicable laws and regulations that directly affect IT operations. First, the requirements for IT service delivery must be considered, including the services of third parties and the effects on the IT organization and its processes and infrastructure. In addition, the laws and regulations relating to electronic data processing, data protection, internal checkpoints, financial reporting, industry-specific regulations, intellectual property and copyright, and even work safety must be evaluated.

Tools

SAP GRC Repository

All regulations and laws, as well as the internal control system derived from them, are stored in the SAP GRC Repository. One type of control documented in the GRC Repository is the check on the segregation of duties, which also can be performed with SAP GRC Access Control. All application-related and IT-related checks are grouped and managed centrally in the SAP GRC Repository. This central storage reduces the costs involved in the audit process, and also makes it possible to immediately identify and remove redundant controls.

Services

SAP Authorization Strategy Concept for SOX Compliance

The result of the *SAP Authorization Strategy Concept for SOX Compliance* service is the identification of all important security deficiencies in the implemented SAP authorization concept. Changes are suggested, and an implementation plan is formulated to remedy these deficiencies.

6.4 ME4: Ensuring IT Governance

The goal of this control is to create reporting that transparently shows whether and how the IT plan was implemented. The most important decision makers from the IT and business fields must be informed whether the planned value potentials have been achieved. In addition, the IT risk after the implementation must be evaluated. A competent assessment must be made as to whether the technical limits have been achieved or even exceeded. The most important goal is to prevent loss of business through IT system failures. Therefore, all the persons responsible must have transparent information as to which IT infrastructure and IT applications can provide stable, failure-free operation for the most important business processes.

Tools

SAP GRC Repository

The SAP GRC Repository centrally documents and stores the information related to all statutory, risk-related, and compliance topics. It manages all GRC content, including frameworks, regulations, processes, and controls, thus ensuring that company regulations and their related infrastructure are mapped consistently, effectively, and efficiently.

Services

SAP Solution Management Assessment

SAP provides the *Solution Management Assessment* service as part of the Premium Engagements, to identify and evaluate availability requirements. In this process, the solution landscape and the most important core business processes are analyzed. The result is a description and a technical evaluation of the risks to stability, as well as the availability and safety of the core business processes.

7   Relevance of CobiT and COSO for Fulfilling SOX

The interrelationships between CobiT, COSO, and SOX were already discussed at the beginning of this pocket guide. SOX is a law in the U.S. that regulates liability for the quality of information and company financial reports. SOX focuses on financial reporting. Although the role of SOX seems to be accepted worldwide, it is currently only legally binding in the U.S. It does apply, however, to foreign companies that are listed on U.S. stock exchanges. In some places, country-specific variants with similar content have been imposed, such as Article 728a of the Swiss Code of Obligations. In the meantime, even companies that are not listed on American stock exchanges are declaring their adherence to SOX, in order to increase their credibility.

The Securities and Exchange Commission (SEC)—the U.S. stock-market supervisory body—recommends the internal control framework published by the Committee of Sponsoring Organizations of the Treadway Commission (COSO) as an internal controlling system. It has become the most widely used framework for companies that wish to or need to adapt to SOX compliance. Although IT is an essential component of most financial reporting today, IT controls are recommended but not obligatory. COSO only provides a few instructions for the design and implementation of IT controls.

CobiT fills this gap and supports you in introducing internal controls for IT governance, forming a category of best practice in this area. Nonetheless, IT organizations still have to decide for themselves which of the credibility requirements of SOX financial reporting affect internal IT controls and result in new requirements.

COSO groups the suggested controls in five components, according to the lifecycle of the development of control processes:

► **Control Environment**
The control environment forms the basis for later internal controls. It defines the fundamental prerequisites for establishing controls.

► **Risk Assessment**
The risk-assessment component comprises the identification and analysis of potential risks at a company. It forms the basis for defining the necessary controls.

► **Control Activities**
Information must be provided reliably and punctually. This necessitates certain activities, which are managed by control activities.

► **Information and Communication**
Information and its communication are of vital importance to a company. Information and communication encompass the controls for analyzing what information is necessary in which parts of a company, and how this

information can be communicated with a minimum of risk.

▶ Monitoring

The monitoring component covers the continuous monitoring of the established controls. A distinction is made between manual and automatic monitoring. IT plays an important role, particularly in the introduction of automatic controls and their monitoring.

CobiT provides similar controls for IT. Figure 7.1 shows the relationship between CobiT, COSO, and Sections 320 and 404 of the Sarbanes-Oxley Act.

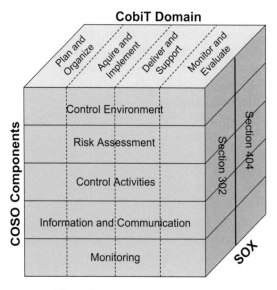

Figure 7.1 Relationships Between CobiT Domains, COSO Components, and SOX

As you can see, there is no direct relationship between COSO components and CobiT domains.

In its publication IT Control Objectives for Sarbanes-Oxley, which was revised in 2006, the IT Governance Institute discussed the relationship between SOX, COSO, and CobiT. The fulfillment of certain control objectives is essential to avoid SOX violations. At the same time, there are no guarantees that adherence to the control objectives will ensure compliance with internal controls in the SOX framework. Given that companies differ in many ways, not only in size and business areas, there is no single strategy for implementing the controls specified by SOX, in the same way that there is no single strategy for implementing CobiT at your company. Every company must determine the optimum mix of suggestions and best practices for itself. To support you in this, the publication IT Control Objectives for Sarbanes-Oxley defines the 12 particularly important IT controls for SOX compliance and their relationships to Auditing Standard No. 2, as published by the Public Company Accounting Oversight Board (PCAOB) (see Table 7.1).

IT Control Objectives for Sarbanes-Oxley	Relationship to CobiT 4.0 process	PCAOB IT General Controls			
		Program development	Program change	System operation	Access to programs and data
1. Acquire and maintain application software	AI2—Acquire and maintain application software	x	x	x	x
2. Acquire and maintain technology infrastructure	AI3—Acquire and Maintain Technology Infrastructure	x	x	x	
3. Enable operation	AI4—Enable Operation and Use	x	x	x	x
4. Install and accredit solutions and changes	AI7—Install and Accredit Solutions and Changes	x	x	x	x
5. Manage changes	AI6—Manage Changes		x		x

Table 7.1 IT Control Objectives for SOX Compliance

#	Control Objective	COBIT Reference				
6.	Define and manage service levels	DS1—Define and Manage Service Levels	X	X	X	X
7.	Manage third-party services	DS2—Manage Third-Party Services	X	X	X	X
8.	Guarantee system security	DS5—Guarantee System Security			X	X
9.	Manage configuration	DS9—Manage Configuration			X	X
10.	Manage problems and incidents	DS8—Manage the Service Desk and Incidents DS10—Manage Problems			X	
11.	Manage data	DS11—Manage Data			X	X
12.	Manage the physical environment and operation	DS12—Manage the Physical Environment DS13—Manage Operation			X	X

Table 7.1 IT Control Objectives for SOX Compliance (contd.)

The IT Governance Institute supports you in selecting the most important controls for your company, by classifying their importance as follows:

▶ **Entity Level**
IT controls that do not require specific actions are categorized under entity level. They are important for understanding the type and significance of internal controls and gaining an overview of the control framework.

▶ **Activity-Level Controls**
Activity-level controls are used to control processes to ensure that the reporting for stockholders, investors, and accountants is conducted using up-to-date, complete, and confidential information. This requires particularly reliable information systems and their stable IT operation.

For an exact list of how COSO and CobiT controls relate to each other, please refer to the corresponding publication of the IT Governance Institute, *IT Control Objectives for Sarbanes-Oxley*.

In spite of all recommendations and guidelines, it remains each company's prerogative to define and implement the measures that are suitable for its particular needs. Controls can be conducted manually or automatically, for example. Even if a business process can be controlled with fully functional software support, and no data inconsistencies have occurred yet, there is no guarantee that the data was actually correct or will remain correct in future. You should therefore design and implement controls without delay and perform them regularly, even if you are not yet obliged to operate according to SOX. In the long term, the confidential exchange of information and reporting will become absolutely vital for all companies.

8 Outlook

In future, SAP will expand its solution set for sustainable corporate governance, risk management, and compliance with regulatory requirements.

SAP plans the initial release of SAP GRC Risk Management for 2007. This product supports customers in the set-up and automatic processing of cross-functional risk-management processes. Central business risks on different company levels are analyzed and integrated across organizational units, processes, and IT systems. Specially developed collaborative procedures support the personnel responsible for identifying financial, legal, and operative risks in sharing information with other business experts in the company. Possible response measures are evaluated in terms of efficiency or achieving a return on investment. Actionable reporting provides all relevant information in its business context for the responsible managers of the IT organization, sales and distribution, or the risk-management department at the company. This ensures that the risks can be evaluated across business areas and that those responsible can react in a suitable manner.

SAP Solution Manager 4.0 has taken SAP's application management platform to a new level of sophistication. Accordingly, this release will be continued until at least 2009 (and possibly longer). To give customers a high degree of planning reliability, plans to issue a new release will be made known at least one year before ramp-up. Figure 8.1 shows SAP's release planning and maintenance strategy for SAP Solution Manager.

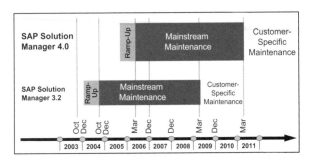

Figure 8.1 SAP Solution Manager Release Planning and Maintenance Strategy

SAP Solution Manager will be continually enhanced (see Figure 8.2) to cover a wide range of other areas:

▸ To ensure that new functions are available to customers in a timely fashion and that the standard functions of SAP Solution Manager are continually improved, enhancements will be supplied using dedicated Support Package Stacks.

▸ All customers who want to integrate products from other providers in the application management area using SAP Solution Manager can use Integration Packages to simplify this process. These integration scenarios for third-party tools can be found in System Management and in the Service Desk, for example.

▶ Customer-segment-specific extensions for SAP Solution Manager 4.0 will be made available in such a form that they can be flexibly integrated in the standard SAP Solution Manager.

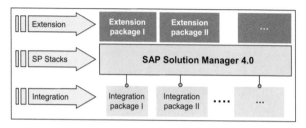

Figure 8.2 Ongoing Development of the SAP Solution Manager 4.0

SAP GRC Risk Management and SAP Solution Manager are not the only tools for the appropriate implementation of CobiT controls, but they do play an important role in this area. Regardless of which tools you use or intend to use, the most important factor is the manner in which your employees experience the processes. Tools can only support processes, and not employees or their collaboration.

A CobiT Controls

The following table shows in detail which CobiT controls are especially important for SOX compliance. The table is based on the publication *IT Control Objectives for Sarbanes-Oxley* from the IT Governance Institute. Chapter 7 explains the priority levels Entity, Activity, and Most Relevant. Which CobiT Controls are most important depends on the size of your company and the kind of business it is. The table could serve as a guideline for implementation of your customer-specific SOX compliance solution.

	Entity Level	Activity Level	Most relevant
PO1 Define a Strategic IT Plan			
PO1.1 IT Value Management			
PO1.2 Business-IT Alignment	x		
PO1.3 Assessment of Current Performance	x		
PO1.4 IT Strategic Plan	x	x	
PO1.5 IT Tactical Plans			
PO1.6 IT Portfolio Management			
PO2 Define the Information Architecture			
PO2.1 Information Architecture Model			

	Entity Level	Activity Level	Most relevant
PO2.2 Enterprise Data Dictionary and Data Syntax Rules			
PO2.3 Data Classification Scheme			
PO2.4 Integrity Management			
PO3 Determine Technological Direction			
PO3.1 Technological Direction Planning			
PO3.2 Technical Infrastructure Plan—Scope and Coverage			
PO3.3 Monitoring of Future Trends and Regulations			
PO3.4 Technology Standards			
PO3.5 IT Architecture Board			
PO4 Define the IT Processes, Organization and Relationships			
PO4.1 IT Process Framework			
PO4.2 IT Strategy Committee		x	
PO4.3 IT Steering Committee			
PO4.4 Organizational Placement of the IT Function			
PO4.5 IT Organizational Structure			
PO4.6 Roles and Responsibilities	x		
PO4.7 Responsibility for IT Quality Assurance			
PO4.8 Responsibility for Risk, Security and Compliance			
PO4.9 Data and System Ownership	x		
PO4.10 Supervision			
PO4.11 Segregation of Duties	x		

	Entity Level	Activity Level	Most relevant
PO4.12 IT Staffing			
PO4.13 Key IT Personnel			
PO4.14 Contracted Staff Policies and Procedures			
PO4.15 Relationships			
PO5 Manage the IT Investment			
PO5.1 Financial Management Framework			
PO5.2 Prioritization Within IT Budget			
PO5.3 IT Budgeting Process			
PO5.4 Cost Management			
PO5.5 Benefit Management			
PO6 Communicate Management Aims and Direction			
PO6.1 IT Policy and Control Environment	x	x	o
PO6.2 Enterprise IT Risk and Internal Control Framework			
PO6.3 IT Policies Management	x	x	o
PO6.4 Policy Rollout			
PO6.5 Communication of IT Objectives and Direction	x	x	o
PO7 Manage IT Human Resources			
PO7.1 Personnel Recruitment and Retention			
PO7.2 Personnel Competencies	x		
PO7.3 Staffing of Roles			
PO7.4 Personnel Training	x		
PO7.5 Dependence Upon Individuals			

	Entity Level	Activity Level	Most relevant
PO7.6 Personnel Clearance Procedures			
PO7.7 Employee Job Performance Evaluation	x		
PO7.8 Job Change and Termination			
PO8 Manage Quality			
PO8.1 Quality Management System	x	x	o
PO8.2 IT Standards and Quality Practices	x	x	o
PO8.3 Development and Acquisition Standards		x	o
PO8.4 Customer Focus			
PO8.5 Continuous Improvement			
PO8.6 Quality Measurement, Monitoring and Review	x		
PO9 Assess and Manage IT Risks			
PO9.1 IT and Business Risk Management Alignment	x		
PO9.2 Establishment of Risk Context	x		
PO9.3 Event Identification	x		
PO9.4 Risk Assessment	x		
PO9.5 Risk Response	x		
PO9.6 Maintenance and Monitoring of a Risk Action Plan	x		
PO10 Manage Projects			
AI1 Identify Automated Solutions		x	o
AI2 Acquire and Maintain Application Software		x	o
AI2.1 High-level Design		x	o

	Entity Level	Activity Level	Most relevant
AI2.2 Detailed Design		x	o
AI2.3 Application Control and Audit-ability		x	o
AI2.4 Application Security and Availability		x	o
AI2.5 Configuration and Implementation of Acquired Application Software			
AI2.6 Major Upgrades to Existing Systems			
AI2.7 Development of Application Software			
AI2.8 Software Quality Assurance			
AI2.9 Application Requirements Management			
AI3 Acquire and Maintain Technology Infrastructure		x	
AI3.1 Technological Infrastructure Acquisition Plan		x	
AI3.2 Infrastructure Resource Protection and Availability		x	
AI3.3 Infrastructure Maintenance		x	
AI3.4 Feasibility Test Environment			
AI4 Enable Operation and Use			
AI5 Procure IT Resources			
AI6 Manage Changes		x	
AI6.1 Change Standards and Procedures		x	o
AI6.2 Impact Assessment, Prioritization and Authorization		x	o
AI6.3 Emergency Changes		x	o

	Entity Level	Activity Level	Most relevant
AI6.4 Change Status Tracking and Reporting		x	o
AI6.5 Change Closure and Documentation		x	o
AI7 Install and Accredit Solutions and Changes			
AI7.1 Training			
AI7.2 Test Plan		x	o
AI7.3 Implementation Plan		x	o
AI7.4 Test Environment		x	o
AI7.5 System and Data Conversion		x	o
AI7.6 Testing of Changes		x	o
AI7.7 Final Acceptance Test		x	o
AI7.8 Promotion to Production		x	o
AI7.9 Software Release		x	o
AI7.10 System Distribution		x	o
AI7.11 Recording and Tracking of Changes		x	o
AI7.12 Post-implementation Review		x	
DS1 Define and Manage Service Levels			
DS1.1 Service Level Management Framework		x	
DS1.2 Definition of Services		x	
DS1.3 Service Level Agreements		x	
DS1.4 Operating Level Agreements			
DS1.5 Monitoring and Reporting of Service Level Achievements		x	

	Entity Level	Activity Level	Most relevant
DS1.6 Review of Service Level Agreements and Contracts		x	
DS2 Manage Third-party Services		x	
DS2.1 Identification of All Supplier Relationships			
DS2.2 Supplier Relationship Management		x	
DS2.3 Supplier Risk Management		x	
DS2.4 Supplier Performance Monitoring			
DS3 Manage Performance and Capacity			
DS4 Ensure Continuous Service			
DS5 Ensure Systems Security			
DS5.1 Management of IT Security			
DS5.2 IT Security Plan		x	o
DS5.3 Identity Management		x	o
DS5.4 User Account Management		x	o
DS5.5 Security Testing, Surveillance and Monitoring		x	o
DS5.6 Security Incident Definition		x	
DS5.7 Protection of Security Technology			
DS5.8 Cryptographic Key Management			
DS5.9 Malicious Software Prevention, Detection and Correction		x	
DS5.10 Network Security		x	
DS5.11 Exchange of Sensitive Data			

	Entity Level	Activity Level	Most relevant
DS6 Identify and Allocate Costs			
DS7 Educate and Train Users			
DS7.1 Identification of education and training needs	x		
DS7.2 Delivery of training and education			
DS7.3 Evaluation of training received			
DS8 Manage Service Desk and Incidents		x	o
DS8.1 Service Desk			
DS8.2 Registration of customer queries			
DS8.3 Incident escalation		x	
DS8.4 Incident closure			
DS8.5 Trend analysis			
DS9 Manage the Configuration			
DS9.1 Configuration repository and baseline			
DS9.2 Identification and maintenance of configuration items		x	
DS9.3 Configuration integrity review			
DS10 Manage Problems			
DS10.1 Identification and classification of problems		x	
DS10.2 Problem tracking and resolution		x	
DS10.3 Problem closure (DS10.3 Abschluss von Problemen)		x	
DS10.4 Integration of change, configuration and problem management			

	Entity Level	Activity Level	Most relevant
DS11 Manage Data			
DS11.1 Business requirements for data management		x	
DS11.2 Storage and retention arrangements		x	
DS11.3 Media library management system			
DS11.4 Disposal			
DS11.5 Backup and restoration		x	o
DS11.6 Security requirements for data management		x	
DS12 Manage the Physical Environment			
DS12.1 Site selection and layout			
DS12.2 Physical security measures		x	
DS12.3 Physical access		x	
DS12.4 Protection against environmental factors			
DS12.5 Physical facilities management			
DS13 Manage Operations			
DS13.1 Operations procedures and instructions		x	o
DS13.2 Job scheduling		x	o
DS13.3 IT infrastructure monitoring		x	
DS13.4 Sensitive documents and output devices			
DS13.5 Preventive maintenance for hardware			

	Entity Level	Activity Level	Most relevant
ME1 Monitor and Evaluate IT-Performance			
ME1.1 Monitoring Approach			
ME1.2 Definition and Collection of Monitoring Data	x		
ME1.3 Monitoring Method			
ME1.4 Performance Assessment	x		
ME1.5 Board and Executive Reporting			
ME1.6 Remedial Actions	x		
ME2 Monitor and Evaluate Internal Control	x		
ME2.1 Monitoring of internal control framework	x		
ME2.2 Supervisory review	x		
ME2.3 Control exceptions			
ME2.4 Control self-assessment			
ME2.5 Assurance of internal control	x		
ME2.6 Internal control at third parties	x	x	o
ME2.7 Remedial actions	x		
ME3 Ensure Regulatory Compliance			
ME3.1 Identification of laws and regulations having potential impact on IT	x		
ME3.2 Optimization of response to regulatory requirements	x		
ME3.3 Evaluation of compliance with regulatory requirements			
ME3.4 Positive assurance of compliance			
ME3.5 Integrated reporting			

	Entity Level	Activity Level	Most relevant
ME4 Provide IT-Governance			
ME4.1 Establishment of an IT governance framework			
ME4.2 Strategic alignment			
ME4.3 Value delivery			
ME4.4 Resource management			
ME4.5 Risk management	x		
ME4.6 Performance measurement			
ME4.7 Independent assurance			

B Literature

► Anderhub, Vital: *Service Level Management—The ITIL Process in SAP Operations*, SAP PRESS Essentials 21, SAP PRESS, Bonn 2006.

► Hopstaken, B.B.A.; Kranendonk, A.: *Informatieplanning: puzzelen met beleid en plan*, Stenford Kroese, Leiden 1988.

► Schulz, Corina: *Conception and Installation of System Monitoring Using the SAP Solution Manager*, SAP PRESS Essentials 2, SAP PRESS, Bonn 2005.

► Schäfer, Marc O.; Melich, Matthias: *SAP Solution Manager*, SAP PRESS, Bonn 2007.

► Evans, Ivor; Macfarlane, Ivor: *A Dictionary of IT Service Management*, The Stationary Office Books, London 2002.

► Brand, Koen; Boonen, Harry: *IT Governance. A Pocket Guide based on CobiT*, Haren Van Publishing, Zaltbommel 2005.

► ISACA: *IT Control Objectives for Sarbanes-Oxley*, 2nd Edition, IT Governance Institute, Rolling Meadows 2006.

► Schöler, Sabine; Will, Liane: *SAP IT Service & Application Management. The ITIL Guide for SAP Operations*, SAP PRESS, Bonn 2006.

Index

**Implementing ITIL Processes
in Your SAP Department**

96 pp., 2006, 19,95 Euro / US$ 29.95
ISBN 978-1-59229-094-9

SAP IT Service & Application Management
www.sap-press.com

S. Schöler, L. Will

SAP IT Service & Application Management

The ITIL Guide for SAP Operations

With this one-of-a-kind pocket guide you learn how
to fill the ITIL processes of IT Service Management
and Application Management with real "SAP life"
and you get recommendations on which SAP tools
and services are available to best support you in this
effort. The integration processes between both areas
are also covered in detail. This is a must-have
reference for IT managers responsible for optimizing
SAP operations and cost structures.

**SOA and the benefits
of the enterprise services
architecture approach**

**Architectural concepts, design
approach, and standards**

**Steps to successfully
deploy ESA**

144 pp., 2006, 49,95 Euro / US$ 49.95
ISBN 1-59229-095-7

Enterprise Services Architecture
for Financial Services

www.sap-press.com

Bruno Bonati, Joachim Regutzki, Martin Schroter

Enterprise Services Architecture for
Financial Services

Taking SOA to the next level

Service-oriented architecture (SOA) has become an
important topic for financial services organizations, offering
new levels of flexibility, adaptability and cost savings. This
book cuts through the confusion by clearly describing SAP's
approach to SOA the enterprise services architecture (ESA),
shared with leading banks and insurance companies. By
illustrating the principles and vision behind ESA, this
invaluable guide shows you exactly how it can benefit your
financial services firm. In a concise andeasy-to-read format,
the authors introduce you toESA and explain exactly how it
works. In addition, you'll get a detailed description of the
key steps that financial services institutions need to take in
order to successfully deploy ESA. This book is written
primarily for CIOs, CTOs, IT managers, andconsultants.